Reading
the
Water

OUTDOOR LIFE TAKE-ALONG BOOKS

Reading the Water

Where and When to Fish in Lakes and Streams

Joseph D. Bates, Jr.

Drawings by Tom Beecham

Outdoor Life · *Harper & Row*

New York · *London*

CONTENTS

INTRODUCTION

It has been said that ten percent of fishermen catch ninety percent of the fish. Since about fifty million people in the United States enjoy fishing, why should about forty-five million of them return home relatively fishless so often?

A key reason may be that the majority doesn't know how to pick the hotspots. Instead of fishing where fish should be, they waste too much time in places no respectable gamefish would bother with. Of course the when-to-fish and the how-to-fish elements enter into it, but the "lucky" ten percent instinctively know how to "read the water"; how to tell productive spots and depths from useless ones.

So this little book will try to condense "where to fish" information and, to round things out a bit, also will include some of the "when to" and the "how to." But, since we can't catch fish unless we're fishing where they should be, the "where to" is the most important.

Excluding for the moment some of the species that make spawning runs up rivers from the sea, the others invariably retain the heritage of several inborn traits endowed by nature in an attempt to keep them out of trouble. Since these traits are rather human ones, let's start out by assuming that fish are a lot more like people than people might suppose.

We prefer temperatures of about 70 degrees and can tolerate those in a wider range, but we try to stay out of excessive heat and cold whenever possible. So do fish. We want to be near a food supply, and fish do, too. We seek places of protection from dangers of various kinds, and we usually want to be where we can rest without much exertion. So do fish. When we find places where these conditions exist, we try to remain there. When we realize that fish also seek similar conditions we can pass by those that don't seem to qualify and can confine our fishing to the "fishy" locations which are bound to be the most productive.

I live in what used to be a small New England town which in recent years has become heavily populated. When my son was about twelve years old I gave him a set of fishing tackle for his birthday and, with it, a briefing on the principal facts of life about catching fish.

The boy promptly disappeared with his tackle and, in an hour or two, returned home with four very respectable trout. Such quick results were rather remarkable hereabouts, even though my son got around on a bicycle.

While Bruce was cleaning his fish I asked him where he had caught them.

"You know what you told me, Dad," he said. "You said for me to stop and think where I'd like to live if I were a fish, and to go there if I wanted to catch one. So I decided that if I were a fish I would like to live in the brook under the country club bridge where it is shady and cool. So I went there and drifted a worm into the culvert. I had only four worms, but each one took a fish!"

"Reading the water" is the ability to decide where fish should be by knowing why they should be there. This is what this book mostly is about. I hope it will help readers to enjoy more successful excursions on lake and stream.

1

READ IT BEFORE YOU FISH

In younger years I was lucky enough to be allowed to go fishing with several older experts, a few of whom eventually became famous. Naturally, I wanted to show them that I was quite a smart operator!

An early deflation came when Herbie Welch took me trout fishing on Maine's Kennebago Stream. I hurriedly rigged up, waded into the water, and started fishing. After a number of unproductive casts, I noticed Herbie still placidly sitting on the bank.

"Why aren't you fishing?" I called to him.

"You come up here and sit down, and I'll tell you why," Herbie said with something of a frown.

He filled his pipe and puffed on it for a minute while gazing over the water.

"Mind if I tell you a couple of things?" he asked. Not waiting for an answer, he started in.

"When you come to a new piece of water you shouldn't just splash in and start throwing your fly or bait all around the place. It's better to look the situation over, and to plan an approach. I call it taking time to 'read the water.' Some other people call it just common horse sense. But take time to figure things out. When you think you've got 'em figured out, then go to it —but not before.

4

"Now what you just did was to splash into the pool right where some of the best fish were. Maybe you noticed 'em scoot away—you should have. What you just did was to drive away or put down every good fish in this part of the pool. So we'll just sit here for half an hour and let 'em get calmed down again while I tell you some of the fishy facts of life!

"Now, just look at this pool," he went on. "Over there the water is shallow, and there's no current of any importance. So forget that part. But over across there is a little bank, and what do you see?"

"Greener grass and bushes," I said, "and maybe the water's a little deeper right there."

Figure 1. A typical spring hole, identified by lush vegetation. Cold water seeps through rocks and gravel to gouge out a hole deeper than normal stream depth. The colder water provides more suitable temperature for fish in summer.

"What you should see is a spring hole, marked by the greener and lusher area and the trickle of water dripping down over the gravel. Now, this is summer, and the water's rather warm, so there should be fish lying in the spring hole, where it is much colder.

Edge Water

"And over there," he pointed, "is a big rock with current pouring around both sides of it. Both sides form edges downstream, with quieter water in between. The deeper edge is the better one, and a trout or two should be there."

"What's an edge?" I asked.

"Best way to explain it is to say that gamefish like trout and landlocked salmon don't lie in the fast current because it's hard for them to hold position there. They like to rest, or hold, in water of moderate flow. What's 'moderate flow'?

"Imagine you're standing in fast water. Put your hand in the water on the upstream side of your waders, and you'll find fast current there; also along the sides of your waders. But put your hand downstream of your waders and you'll notice that your leg obstructs the flow to provide a small bit of quiet water. On each side of this little patch of quiet water is a dividing line between the fast and the quiet water. This dividing line is called an 'edge,' and you can see it as the current streams around your leg. Of course there are two edges, and fish in fairly deep water should be lying in the areas of moderate flow just inside of each edge.

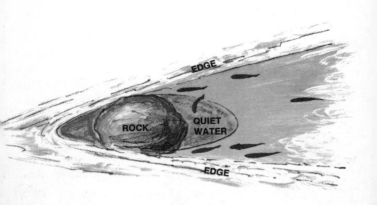

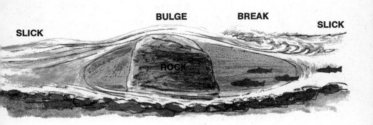

Figure 2. Holding water around a rock in a stream. Dividing line between fast and quiet water, shown by dotted lines, is called an "edge." Favorite holding places for trout are just inside of edge water near the bottom. Quiet water in front of and behind the rock also may contain fish.

"This is what happens when rocks or a bridge abutment or anything else obstructs the fast flow of a stream current. The stream flows around the obstruction and forms two trailing edges below it, with quiet water in between. If the water is deep enough, or if the rock provides protection, fish should be holding along the edges or perhaps in the quiet water in between.

"And the current scoops out a hole down-stream of the rock, and sometimes, if the rock is big enough and if the current is right, up-stream of it, so it makes nice hiding and resting places for fish. When you see a big rock in the current, fish just upstream of it, and then fish the edges as far down as the current breaks. Even if fish are behind a big rock, they are watching the edges for food coming down, and they will see your fly or bait if you fish it deep enough. In fairly deep water you may have to get the line down, close to the bottom. Some-times, when fish are lying in deep water, they can't see a lure fished too shallow, or maybe they won't bother to come up for it.

"Now, we've talked long enough. Wade out to casting distance of the spring hole and fish it; first fairly far away, then with succeeding casts closer. Wade slowly and quietly—no splashing! Cast a bit upstream so the current will sweep your fly down deep into the hole."

I did as he said and on the second cast hooked a trout over a foot long. Putting all the tension on him that seemed safe, I drew him into the pool hoping other fish in the hole hadn't been disturbed. The colorful brook trout of Maine are fat and full of fight. After he had made a few splashing swirls and strong rushes I led him to the net. Later, I put the fly closer into the hole and caught another. Since then, on lake or stream, I always keep an eye out for spring holes when the rest of the water is warm.

While we boiled coffee and toasted sandwiches on forked sticks over a small fire, Herbie con-tinued the discussion.

Holding Water vs. Feeding Water

"Can you tell holding water from feeding water?" he asked. I admitted I had only a vague idea about it.

"First, about holding water," he said. "You can call it 'resting water,' if you want to. It's the kind of water fish stay in when they're not actively feeding.

"Holding water should have several characteristics, of which four are important. It's better if all four exist in the same place, but they all don't necessarily have to. One is protection from observation and enemies. This is provided by such things as rocks, ledges, fallen trees or stumps in the water, undercut banks and, in certain places like limestone or hard-water streams, by weeds or grasses, whose long fronds in flowing water often are in dense masses trailing downstream. Protection probably is the most important characteristic of holding water. Maybe next is depth, such as places in deep pools, but fish often will hold in rather shallow, cool water. We have discussed the importance of moderate flow. In streams, you'll rarely find gamefish in dead water, or in very fast water, unless they are traveling or feeding. Finally, it's good to have a disturbed surface—ripples, waves, or white water, that is. Where water conditions disturb the surface, fish evidently think they can't be seen. Remember these four characteristics. Where you notice all four of them the place should be a hotspot. If there are less than four, it may still be worth a try.

"So holding water is water where fish think they can't be seen and where they can rest in comfort. It may be even such simple places as spots near the bank where something casts shadows on the water. I've seen trout lying over submerged leaves and in grasses on the bottom. Their protective coloration makes them almost invisible, and I guess they know it.

"Feeding water, on the other hand, is water where fish can be seen, such as in the riffles, or over the gravel of a pool. The water may have a glassy surface. Fish venture into it to feed, usually on the nymphs in the gravel, the baitfish swimming around, or whatever the current brings down to them.

"Gamefish move to feeding water usually after sundown or during the night but, if there are insect hatches or other reasons, they may feed anytime during the day, especially when the sun is off the water. Sometimes you can see them rising, or tailing—an indication that they are feeding.

"Of course, feeding water and holding water can be the same thing. Fish lying in protected water of moderate flow may not need to travel to open stretches to find food. They get enough from what the current brings down."

Herbie took a last swallow of coffee, and lighted his pipe.

Where Fish Aren't

"Now, we've discussed where gamefish should be in streams," he said. "Let's talk about where they shouldn't be.

"They shouldn't be in water with a muddy or sandy bottom, because there's no protection or food—no reason to be there. They shouldn't be in the thin, flat stretches of a stream because, unless there are rocks or there is some other kind of protection, they can be seen too easily. Where streams flatten out the food supply also is too widely scattered. Look for fish where currents concentrate the drifting food supply into fairly narrow paths.

"So far, we've talked only about gamefish, and on most rivers this usually refers to members of the trout and char families. In their living and feeding habits, all members of these species have such similar characteristics that we can lump them together, at least for a start. They all seek places in rivers offering protection, depth, moderate flow and usually a disturbed surface, although some kinds may want one characteristic more than others.

"One very important thing we haven't touched on is that fish need an ample oxygen supply. They need it more when water is warm than when it is cold. During warm-water periods less oxygen is dissolved in the water, so look for fish where the water is aerated by rapids, waterfalls, and incoming brooks, or where there is a lot of aquatic vegetation, which of course absorbs carbon dioxide and releases oxygen.

"Smallmouth bass sometimes are found in rivers, but they prefer the quiet water of pools to fast-moving currents. When I was a kid I used to enjoy fishing for chubs, mainly because I could catch so many of them. Often they are found in quiet moving water which also sometimes is frequented by trout, and they take trout lures, baits, and flies so often that they can become a nuisance. The trout fisherman who catches chubs should go somewhere else, because he is not fishing in prime trout water. Many fishermen who are beginners often get excited because they see a bunch of suckers in quiet pools and think they are trout. If these men were better water readers they would realize that trout do not lie in dead water where they can so easily be seen. They are much too smart for that!"

As we walked toward the car I said, "Water reading seems to be a good term for using common sense in fishing—in deciding where fish should be so you won't have to waste time fishing where they shouldn't be. But aren't there other factors which are involved, such as barometric pressure and temperature, for instance?"

"We were talking about how to locate the good fishing spots in a stream so we can avoid the others," Herbie said. "On the matter of barometric pressure, most anglers think fish bite best when the barometer is steady or rising, and probably there's something to it. But I say that you don't stay home watching the barometer and reading tables about the time of the day or the week or month when fishing should be best. You go fishing when you have the time to go and, if you know how to use your tackle and how to read the water, you probably will enjoy a good day of it."

Water Temperature

While he took his rod down and pulled his waders off he added, "On water temperature— that really is important because it helps to tell you where to fish and it tells you whether you can fish on or near the surface, or whether you must fish deeper down. All species of fish are most active at a certain water temperature, and they are inclined to hit best at that temperature. They go where their favorite temperature exists, if they can. Of course they tolerate a range a bit higher and lower than that, but they may not bite as well. The favorite water temperatures of various species of fish vary somewhat, and we know what they are. I guess part of reading the water is knowing what the ideal temperature is, and going to places fish should be in because that temperature exists there. A water thermometer should be in every fisherman's tacklebox, as well as a little chart giving the favorite temperature ranges of the kinds of fish he wants to catch. We'll fish trout lakes and bass lakes later, and learn more about it!"

2

WHERE TO FIND FISH IN RIVERS

We parked the car near the bridge and walked on to it to look at the water. It ran deep and dark before spilling over the dam into the pool below. The banks were thickly bushed, but paths to the stream, rusty worm cans and Y-cut sticks beside it indicated frequent visits by bait fishermen.

"The mile downstream from this bridge," Herbie said, "is one of my favorite stretches because it contains most of the typical holding and feeding positions found on all small to medium streams everywhere. I drew a map of the stream and had several copies made. Here's one for you. Let's discuss it as we fish it. (*See Figure 3, pages 16 and 17.*)

"This deep run above, under, and just below the bridge (**A**) is an excellent spot because it provides depth, moderate flow, and protection. It is fished often by people sinking worms to the bottom and waiting for something to happen. We won't bother with it. If we did, the trick is to drift the bait down deep, letting it travel naturally with the current. The bait must look natural and must drift naturally. A wobbling spoon, because it can be fished deeper, would be better than a spinner here. If we used wet flies or nymphs we would try to fish them along the bottom on a sinking line.

"Of course this pool (**B**) also is fished a lot, so trout mostly lie under the dam where it's almost impossible to get at them. If this place is good at all, it's good only at daybreak and near dark. I don't like to fish so near the road because roadside locations invariably are too heavily fished. At dark fishermen usually stand on the ledge and try to work their lures deep as near the dam as possible. The eddy on the other side is chub and sucker water. In a less popular place there should be trout above and below the rocks (**C**) but here they probably would be small ones, if any. If this pool wasn't fished so much I would wade out below the eddy and fish toward the side where the ledge is, because that's where most of the current goes. You've got to get your lure down deep here. In a pool like this the water between the rocks and the riffle would be good feeding water, especially late in the evening. The water below the riffle would be good feeding water, too.

"We have seen how rocks in the current make moderate flow. These three big ones (**D**) provide six edges, and there are more rocks under water—a fine holding position for fish."

We walked downstream on the field side.

"Below the rocks is flat water (**E**) with no place for big fish to hide. This isn't holding water but, when the river is moderately high, it can be good feeding water, mainly because of its gravel bottom. No fish are rising or tailing now; no sign of anything going on, so we'll pass it by.

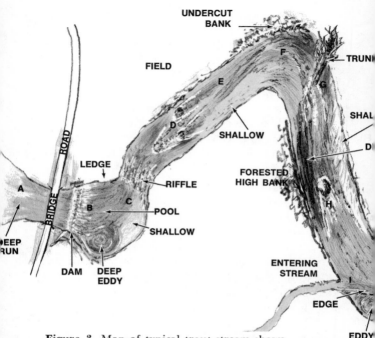

Figure 3. Map of typical trout stream shows the various kinds of water usually encountered. See text for full explanation of how to fish each situation.

Undercut Bank

"Now we come to a real hotspot; a deep run (**F**) with an undercut bank. A big one, or several of them, should be lying under the bank. Fishermen usually fish this spot from this side. When they walk on the bank, fish can hear them. This is enough of a warning for them not to take a lure, even if it looks good. It is better to fish this place from the other side. If the water

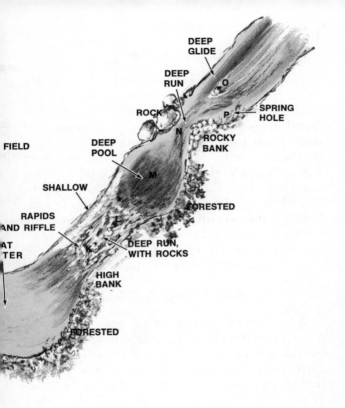

FIELD

DEEP GLIDE

DEEP RUN

ROCK

O

SPRING HOLE

N

P

ROCKY BANK

DEEP POOL

M

SHALLOW

FORESTED

RAPIDS AND RIFFLE

AT TER

DEEP RUN, WITH ROCKS

K

HIGH BANK

FORESTED

is cold and there's no sign of surface activity, wade out above the point on the other side and work the lure deep, as nearly under the bank as possible.

"In summer this is a beautiful dry-fly spot. Insects in the grassy overhanging sod drop into the water. There's a swirl you almost can't see because of the current, and the insect is gone. If no hatch is obvious, I would try a dry fly that imitates an insect, such as a grasshopper or a bee.

Log in Water

"Now just below here is the kind of spot I always enjoy; maybe because it's sort of a challenge. The trunk (**G**) of a big dead elm has tipped over and fallen into the water. Logs and other floating matter have been caught above it. First work your lure as close to the upstream side of the log as possible. Trout should be lying under the log, watching for something to eat. Cast close to the floating debris, too. If that doesn't work, try drifting the lure deeper, under the log and debris. You may lose a lure or two, but it's worth the risk. You can wade out from the shallow side, but don't wade too close!

Forested Bank and Rock

"The current swings from here across the stream, so the field side is the one to fish from. On the other side is a forested high bank, with the water nicely shaded in the afternoon. Don't bother with the shallow side. The fish will be in the deep run along the far shore. You know how to fish the rock (**H**). There should be a couple of good ones near the edges below the rock; especially near the edge on the far side.

Entering Stream

"An entering stream (**I**) can be a hotspot, especially in the summer when the river water is warm. The stream or brook runs cold, so fish will lie in the cool water running out from it. Look carefully to see if there is a drop-off where the brook enters. If so, fish should be lying in the deep water of the drop-off.

"There's a thing about entering streams that most people don't seem to realize," Herbie went on. "You'll notice that just below the stream mouth there is the swirl of an eddy. This forms an edge (dotted line) with the water from the entering stream, and of course it is the eddy that forms the edge. Look carefully and you can see the currents that make it. This is a fine spot for fish to lie, well down past the eddy. Don't bother fishing the eddy; it is chub and sucker water."

"I've caught trout in eddies," I ventured. "Don't they cruise around in such places?"

"Not ordinarily," Herbie said. "You may have taken trout in an eddy because they have followed the lure there. I don't think they were there in the first place.

"Interesting thing about edges," he added. "You'll find them in other places, too. Look for an edge where the two parts of a river meet below an island. Look for one where the water from a shelving riffle meets the main part of the stream. Edges form the condition of moderate flow, and thus are good holding positions for fish, especially if they also offer protection.

"But what may be moderate flow for one species of fish may not be quite so for another. Brook trout and cutthroat trout like it really moderate. Rainbow trout enjoy a faster current, but still not too fast. Brown trout like it quite slow. In the streams he goes to the angler probably knows what species he is likely to catch, so he estimates moderate flow to suit that species. It's not a very critical matter!"

We walked down farther, rounding the bend of the stream.

Flat Water

"This (**J**) is all flat water," said Herbie, quickening his pace a bit. "It's much like the stretch (**E**) above; no places for concealment and very little food, except on the bottom. When the river is over a foot deep here and if a good insect hatch is on, trout may come up from the holding water below to feed over the gravel. It's no good now.

"Strange thing about wide, flat stretches like this," Herbie emphasized. "The water flows smoothly, with no swirls or crests to indicate rocks underneath. Quite obviously there is little depth and no cover, yet we see fishermen wasting hours carefully working over such spots. Without enough depth or cover, so fish can't be seen, there is no reason for them to be in such places unless they are feeding. If they are feeding, in early morning or late evening, you could see them tailing if the water is shallow, or rising if it is deeper. A fisherman can save lots of time and enjoy much better results if he knows how to tell feeding water from holding water. Let's move along."

At the end of the flat water the river narrowed a bit and poured over a short, rapid stretch into a deeper run below a high bank. The stretch held many large rocks, most of which were under water.

Rapids and Riffle

"Now, here's an interesting place," Herbie said. "Let's sit down and rest a bit and look it over. If fish were feeding you might find more of them at the end of the flat water, just above the rapids (**K**). Their holding positions would be in the deep run on the high bank side of the riffle. You could fish this place best by wading down the riffle, which also could be called a bar, and casting across right to the high bank. It's no good on the shallow side."

Deep Run

"That deep run (**L**) is pretty fast," I ventured. "There is so much white water that it's hard to see all the rocks below. Would trout, except possibly for rainbows, hold in such a place?"

"Maybe I should have said this before," Herbie answered, "because it's a very important part of water reading. You can't judge a spot like this by what you see on top. The water near the surface always is the fastest. Under it are many big rocks. These rocks break up the flow, so the water going by the rocks is much slower —an excellent set of holding positions. Trouble is that the fish lie deep, in complete safety. You must work your lure as deep as possible for them, at the same time trying to fish it as naturally as possible. A spinner won't go deep enough, but a weighted fly or a fairly heavy spoon might. If you're fishing bait, allow enough slack line to get it down. Cast quartering downstream and pull your rod back before the fly lands, to provide some slack. When the line straightens, let the fly swing with the current. Casting a bit upstream will get it down even deeper.

Figure 4. A fast-water stretch may look unpromising, but fish lie deep in the slower currents near the edges of the rocks. Weighted wet flies or other sinking lures are recommended.

"Lots of fishermen will try a stretch like this and won't catch anything. On western streams, especially in fishing for steelhead, the experts know they've got to feel the lure bumping bottom occasionally. Steelhead won't go very far to the lure. You must take it down to them.

"Here in the East the same thing is true, especially when water is very cold in the spring. The cold water, at the lower range of their tolerable limits, makes fish dull and logy. A lure drifting very far above them is ignored. If it drifts right to them, they may have enough ambition to take it."

Herbie stood up and stretched. "We're nearly to the end of my favorite part of the river," he said, "and it's about time to start fishing instead of talking about it. But first, let's look at a few other places.

Deep Pool and Run

"Many times, I've sat for an hour or two watching this deep pool (M)," he said. "You can't see the rocks on the bottom very clearly, but fish hold there. Others run up or drop back down to feed. This is better feeding water than holding water, but it's a little of both. Great place for dry-fly fishing in the summer. I've often seen several big ones cruising around the pool; sometimes rising to insects, but usually seeking minnows. A small streamer or bucktail, fished deep, might get results now. You should fish quietly and keep as well hidden as possible. Don't pick up your flyline until it has swung over near the bank. Then strip in as much as possible before you cast again so you won't dis-

turb the water. If you should be using spinning
or spincasting tackle, cast across at the top of the
pool and let the line swing down and through.
Short casts first, followed by longer ones. The
tail of the pool, down near the big rocks, is a
hotspot when fish are feeding.

"Here," Herbie pointed, "is a deep run (**N**),
more or less like a chute between the rocks.
Give it a try, if you want, but it's hard to pre-
sent a lure properly there. You'll notice that
just below the big rocks the run widens out into
a deep glide, with many rocks down deep and a
few breaking water. This is a holding position,
and by now you know how to fish it; especially
the edges streaming back from the rock (**O**) out
near the middle."

A grin came over Herbie's tanned face,
wrinkled by the crow's feet of many summers.
"What do you see on the far bank, across from
the midstream rock?" he asked.

Spring Hole

"By golly, you can't catch me a second time,"
I laughed. "I can see cold water running down
from the bank. It's a spring hole. Mind if I
fish it?"

"The water's pretty cold for trout to be in
there now," Herbie answered. "Give it a try
anyway, and work your lure around the rock on
the retrieve. I'm going downstream about a hundred yards, and will follow you up. If you take
about two hours to fish back to the car you'll be
there by dark. If it's not dark then, fish the run
by the bridge. It should be good for a fish at
that time in the evening. I'm not going to take

Figure 5. Deep runs provide good holding water. In addition to the run in the foreground, extending downstream from the right bank, the edges and positions below the rocks offer excellent holds for fish.

any trout so, if you want to keep a couple, we can use them for dinner."

It was nearly dark when Herbie returned to the car. I had two nice trout and had released several others. "I also took a few smallmouth bass," I said. "They weren't very big, and of course I released them."

Bass

"In these northeastern rivers," Herbie replied, "bass usually are not very big; not enough of the right kinds of food for them, I guess. Around here, bass mostly are lake and pond fish. In the rivers you'll find them in many of the places we've talked about as being good for trout. They like slow water, deep holes, and places below drop-offs. You'll find them in pockets and where floating debris collects, around weed beds, and sometimes at the heads and tails of riffles. They can stand warmer and more discolored water than trout can. Mostly, they hang around near the bottom, no matter how deep the water is, usually moving into shallower water in the evening to feed.

"I surely like bass fishing," Herbie continued. "You'll find good largemouth bass fishing all over the United States, but especially in ponds and lakes, rather than in rivers. Smallmouth bass are widely prevalent east of the Mississippi except in very hot regions of the deep South. In many places, float trips are very popular—drifting down a lazy river and casting to spots such as we've been talking about."

"Once I fished Silver Creek, in Idaho," I said. "It wasn't at all like the fishing we have here.

The river was filled with long bunches of grasses, anchored to the bottom and trailing downstream to the surface, or nearly so. The stream was gravel, two or three feet deep. Wading through the dense bunches of grasses was quite a problem."

"Rivers like that are similar in a way to the limestone streams in places like Pennsylvania," Herbie said, "—full of aquatic vegetation of one kind or another. Most all of it is both holding and feeding water; all slowly flowing, with protection provided by vegetation instead of rocks. In such streams you don't look for holding and feeding water, because it's all about the same. You usually make no random casts, because you'll hook up in the grass. You watch for where a good fish is rising, and you cast to him. Keeping him out of the grass is your problem. When a hatch is on you'll be surprised to see how many fish there are, rising to insects in every open spot in the river. Take plenty of small flies. You'll leave most of 'em in fish or in the grass."

Herbie started the car and backed out on the road, the headlights now shining brightly.

"It's been a great day," I said appreciatively, "and I learned a great deal. Let's stop at the drive-in just ahead. Some hot coffee would taste good!"

Sea-Run Fish

Most rivers, excluding those containing abundant aquatic growth, fortunately offer very similar water-reading characteristics to anglers regardless of where they are located. The stream we have discussed was placed in the Northeast, but it could have been one of the famous steelhead rivers of the West, or a renowned trout stream such as the Madison in Montana or the Gunnison in Colorado. Many coastal rivers are highways for sea-run fish such as Atlantic salmon, shad, silver and chinook salmon, steelhead and sea-run trout.

Steelhead, the rainbow trout that matures in the sea, run up northern Pacific coastal rivers all year long; the timing of the runs being individual with the rivers. Western anglers divide the runs into "winter fish" and "summer fish," the former being prevalent in the rivers generally from December through March, and the latter in the summer and fall. The season for winter fish is the rainy period when rivers are high and fast-flowing. During the summer runs the streams run shallower and more slowly. Therefore, fishing tactics for the two periods are handled rather differently.

The high and fast water common to the winter runs makes it difficult to fish a fly deeply enough and slowly enough because the steelhead are close to the bottom. Therefore, spinning tackle is popular, with lines in the twelve-pound-test range, and plenty of lead to make the lure or bait bump bottom. Leads, often of the pencil type, may weigh about half an ounce, and they are attached to the line with lighter monofilament so they can be broken off when they become caught on the bottom. The connection often includes a three-way swivel. Baits or lures include salmon eggs or clusters or their imitations, and wobbling spoons. If one doesn't become caught on the river bottom once or twice during every dozen casts or so, he isn't fishing deep enough. To catch fish under such conditions, bumping bottom is a necessity. Due to the cold water, steelhead take lures slowly, and one needs a sensitive rod when using baits.

Along with the steelhead, or separately from their runs, anglers also can catch silver and chinook salmon and sea-run cutthroat trout.

During summer runs the rivers are shallower and more placid. While spinning lures then also are effective (usually without lead) experienced anglers often prefer the flyrod, with highly colored flies predominantly in red, yellow and white combinations. Some favorite flies, however, are more drab, the popular ones usually being decided by veteran anglers, who also are fly dressers, on each individual river. Patterns are sparsely dressed to make them sink readily, and wings usually are mounted high to make them pulsate actively in the current.

Since the fish normally lie deep, sinking flylines, or floating lines with sinking tips, are appropriate. One wades into the river at the head of a run and casts the fly to increasing distances, each time letting it swing in an arc downstream. When it begins to hang downstream the idea is to give it several seductive twitches, because a big steelhead may be following or eyeing it and will come up and hit it when he notices a change of action. After a few casts (which should not be so many that one holds up the progress of those wading behind him), the angler slowly wades down the bar or pool, fishing the productive water on whichever side it may be.

Figure 6. Perfect steelhead water on Oregon's Klamath
River. The best spot is the deep run along the far bank,
but submerged rocks in moderate flow also offer good
holding positions.

This method of angling is very similar to that used for Atlantic salmon in the northeast; for rainbow trout, which frequent feeding lanes in many rivers, and for other species.

Normally, the fish follow the same route through each channel, riffle, and pool, resting in the same spots unless the river's bed has been altered by high water. Thus, if one takes a fish in a certain spot, he can be fairly sure that another one will be holding in the same place shortly afterward. The successful angler learns how to locate good holding water.

We occasionally discuss "holding water" or "holding positions" and "feeding water" or "feeding positions," and it is very important to be able to distinguish one type from the other.

Holding water is water in which fish can hide because of protection offered by undercut banks, rocks, ledges, weed growths, submerged fallen trees or brush. Deep pools also provide protection. In streams, this usually is water of moderate flow. It can include swift riffles, swirling glassy runs, fast-moving pools, slicks above rapids where the stream spreads out below pools, long stretches of uniform flow (especially near steep banks) and protected moving water near ledges or in the edges provided by submerged boulders.

Feeding water, on the other hand, provides sources of food, but it need not offer protection. In streams, it usually is where fish can be seen, such as shallow parts of pools where the water may have a glassy surface, or riffles where food is abundant amid rocks and gravel.

When holding water also offers abundant food it may be feeding water as well, as in the case of rivers or streams containing abundant aquatic growth, or lily pad areas of ponds and lakes. When fish need to leave holding water to go to feeding water for food they usually do this near dark or during the night when exposure in such places presumably will go undetected.

Since rocky or gravel bottoms harbor a food supply, these can be good feeding positions. Since sandy or muddy bottoms usually provide little or no food, they rarely are good feeding positions and, unless very deep, are not good holding positions.

In the case of steelhead and most other gamefish, extremely fast water—so fast that it can't be waded—usually is not productive. Dead water, or water flowing slowly, usually is unsuitable. The angler looks for moderate flow, particularly in areas containing good holding positions.

3

SECRETS OF SUCCESS IN BROOKS

One of the best trout fishermen I know rarely fishes big rivers, or even little ones. Small brooks are his specialty. When one sees how small they are, his sanity might be questioned if it were not for his reputation for consistent success.

On a typical day we stopped near a small bridge under which flowed a brook so narrow and overhung with grasses that it seemed to disappear in the meadow beyond. One could step from bank to bank at almost any point. Ignoring my dubious expression he rigged an eight-foot flyrod and tied a small, fat bee made of clipped deer hair (alternating black and yellow bands, and grey hairwings) to his four-pound-test tippet.

"Rig up," he urged. "There are some good trout in here."

I rigged up, but decided to watch him for a while. This was something different!

"You can't let the fish see you, and you must be very quiet," he cautioned. "Creep through the grass and sneak up to the brook and cast the bee to the edge of the grass, twitching it on to the water if you can. I use a long rod to help me reach out farther because you can't cast far here."

While I watched he slithered through the meadow to brookside and deftly dropped his lure in the slit between the grasses which was all one could see of the brook. After casting (if one can use the term here) he gradually lowered the rod tip to obtain a short float. On the second or third try he struck a fish and brought it to the bank. It was a fat and colorful brook trout, at least ten inches long.

After killing the fish he slipped it into a plastic bag and, rolling this up, tucked it into his game pocket. "Now, let's see what you can do," he challenged.

Cutting through the field I took a position farther down. On hands and knees the last few feet I finally reached the cut of the brook and dropped in the bee he had provided. After letting it float as long as the drift would allow, I drew it back and cast again a bit farther down. The fly caught in the grass hanging over the brook, but a slight twitch dropped it into the water. A trout took it instantly. After I took two and released several more, the little stream became more open and trickled over gravel. Not a trout was in sight in the open water, but I hooked another under the bank in a hole made by the roots of a tree.

My companion was walking toward the car, so I crossed the field to join him.

"Is the fishing here always this good?" I asked.

"Usually you can take 'em all season through, from opening day to late fall," he said. "The brook always is cold and, being fed by springs up in the woods, it's always about the same depth. Fishermen don't bother with it because it looks too small, but I come here a few times every season and always have taken several nice fish. There are a few holes that are hotspots, and of course I've found them. The brook practically flows under that big maple tree. There's a nice hole there, but it is unnoticeable because of the bushes. Hard spot to fish, but all you need is a drift of five feet or so. Now, let's try another place."

"Few people realize the secret of meadow brooks," he remarked as he put his rod in the car and his fish in a cooler. "Many have undercut banks, and there's a lot more fishing area in them than appears on the surface. Some are spawning brooks. Rainbows come up from the river in the spring and brown trout and brook trout come up in the fall because these are their spawning periods. But trout live in such brooks all year long, and are relatively undisturbed.

Figure 7. Undercut banks in a brook conceal wider water beneath, often holding good-sized trout.

"When rivers are high and muddy in the spring, trout come into the brooks. When rivers are low and warm in the summer, trout come into the brooks. The average fisherman usually fishes the larger streams. The smart ones forget the streams when they aren't right, and they try the brooks. Of course all brooks are not meadow brooks with undercut banks, but a little prospecting around should locate a few almost anywhere. Part of 'reading the water' is to know when to fish it. If your reading says 'don't fish here now—it's no good,' you skip that place and find a better one. If fishermen were better water readers they would know that there nearly always is protection, moderate flow, and cool water in these little brooks, and that trout usually are in them."

"I always thought that little brooks held too many small fish," I said. "I hate to hurt the little ones. I'm surprised I didn't catch more of the small ones."

"That's why I gave you the bee," he replied. "It's a fat fly on a number six hook. Sometimes I even use a number four. A little trout can't get it into his mouth. Only the keepers can. You may have felt a good many light taps on the fly. Those were small trout. The fly is big enough so that when they try to take it, they can't, and they don't bother any more because by then they know it's not the real thing. The big ones can take it, all right!

"Now, we'll try a different kind of a brook," he said as we drove along. "You are a big-water man. You never bothered much with brooks, except perhaps when you were a kid. I'm quite the contrary. I'm sort of a 'brook nut.' I've fished brooks for over forty years. By now, I guess you could call me an expert!"

"Why do you get such a kick out of fishing brooks?"

"Well, in the first place, there's practically no competition. I have the place to myself. I fish the hard places that most everyone else passes by. It's pretty easy when you know how. The confined casting, or 'dapping,' if you want to call it that, is a challenge. Sneaking up on the water is a challenge. It's unusual fishing, and I think it's fascinating."

"Give me the first part of the lesson verbally," I requested.

"All right. We are going to a bigger brook flowing through very dense undergrowth. In such a brook I fish downstream while many anglers fish upstream. In fishing upstream you splash too much. It scares the fish before you can get to them. I put on boots, or maybe waders, and I get right in the brook. Others fish from the bank, and have to go around the dense parts; the best parts."

"In fishing down," I said, "don't you mess up the stream by washing dirt down ahead of you?"

"That's part of the secret. Sure, I do. I even kick the gravel a bit, and scuff it up occasionally. Dirt going downstream signals to fish that a bank has caved in, or something like that, and they think food might be coming down, so they start looking for it. Scuffing the gravel dislodges nymphs and crawfish and shrimps, or whatever is in the gravel. It starts minnows moving around. It puts the fish on the feed. You can wade downstream quietly, much more so than upstream. You only need a few feet of line. You saw me using an eight-footer in the meadow, and you know why. But in bushy streams I use a short, light rod. You can poke a short one around in the brush easier. All you need is a few feet of drift, and it's not hard to flip the bait or fly into dark holes and under stumps, or to let it down toward brush piles.

"The methods of brook fishing have the same water-reading principles as in river fishing, only you do it in minature. A little rock you wouldn't bother with in a big stream will hold a trout back of it in a small one. Put the lure back of every rock of football size, or even smaller. Fish every dark hole and every little deep run where the stream bottom tilts a bit. Watch for patches of dead leaves on the bottom where it is shady. Trout often lie over them, and you usually can't see them until you get too close and scare them away."

"Do you always use flies?"

"In summer, when insects are out, my bee is a favorite; also grasshoppers or any other fly that imitates a flying insect—flies that are good floaters; not the little duns and variants you'd use in open water. Since you can't false cast, it's too hard to dry them. At the beginning and end of the season a small minnow-like streamer or bucktail works well.

"I'm not above using worms," he added. "Worm fishing is more of an art than the fly fishermen want to admit it is. Then, I use small worms and small hooks. I hook the worm only once, so it will look natural, not all bunched up.

Figure 8. Even the most unlikely looking runs and riffles in a small brook may hold trout. Best spot here is the deep, shaded run under the alders in the left foreground.

I try to give it a natural drift. I don't use night-crawlers, usually. They are too big for trout in brooks. Of course the small worm and small hook may take small trout. If so, I use a larger worm and hook; one that the baby trout can't take so easily and, if they do, one they can't swallow, so they can be released without damage."

"Of course some of our brooks aren't like many in the West," I said. "There, lots of them are rocky, with very fast water pouring down mountains; or brooks in beaver meadows, or brooks running through swamps, like you find in the South."

"But it's all the same principle," the brook fisherman said. "In the rocky, fast water you would look for deep runs, remembering that you have to bounce the bait on the bottom, and that the current below is slower than that on top. You would look for areas of moderate flow back of boulders, and you would look for deep pools. In beaver meadows and swamps you would find deep holes, and you would find undercut banks somewhat like on the meadow brook we just left. It's all the same principle no matter where you are. You read the water to find the fishy spots, and they are very much the same in every type of brook everywhere."

We stopped by a small wooden bridge.

"I'm going to drop you off here," my partner said. "About a mile downstream you'll come to another bridge. I'll park the car there and will be back at dark. You know where I hide the key."

I edged my way through dense brush that separated the field from the brook, and finally was in it. It varied from shallow to knee-deep, and the bushes almost met in a canopy overhead. There was no sign of anyone having been in this part, but I had noticed that the usual rusty bait cans littered the open area by the bridge.

"Only a damn fool would try to fish this," I grumbled to myself, but I decided to do my best anyway. It was only an hour or so until dark.

My rod was a little six-footer and, after a bit of experimentation, I found it fairly easy to flip the bee out and to steer it in a short drift of six feet or so. After retrieving it, low, short roll-casts or arrow-casts would drop the bee on a slack line into every spot that seemed to offer concealment for trout.

There was a dark run along the edge of the right bank. As soon as the fly landed there a trout swirled and tightened. I let him thrash around, trying to steer him from branches and roots where he could become tangled. He was dark-backed, with a white belly and bright spots; nearly a foot long. I kept him as evidence of my success.

Farther down, a boulder broke into the brook. As the bee drifted around it, a swirl from back of the rock indicated another strike. This was a fish of about the same size, and I kept him, too.

Here and there small trout would try to take the bee, but usually they were unsuccessful. Those that had the barb were easily shaken off. My interest in the little brook increased as the minutes went by. All was quiet, wet, and mossy, with lush wild flowers and ferns growing here and there. Several birds became so friendly that they must have thought my presence of no more concern than that of a mink, muskrat, or 'coon.

The two trout I had caught, plus the two from the meadow brook, were enough. During the mile to the bridge I took several more, and released them. My partner had the car door open to provide light while he poured coffee from a Thermos into a cup. My grin of greeting told him all he wanted to know. I put the trout in the cooler and accepted some coffee.

"Convinced?" he asked.

"One of the best days I ever enjoyed," I said truthfully. "I'm glad most people think these brushy brooks are too tough to fish. They will be among my favorite places from now on!"

Brooks vary in character more than rivers do, and this may be part of their challenge. Many are shallow riffly ones flowing through open spaces over gravel, with occasional larger rocks breaking the surface. Here, it helps to wear subdued colors and to avoid quick motions. One can fish a longer floating line with a longer leader, and can probe every pocket and shallow run from a distance that won't frighten the trout. Uncautious anglers catch mostly small fish, but cautious ones know that even the smallest, most unlikely looking riffles, runs, and pockets may hold trout of surprisingly large size.

This lesson was pegged into my mind after fishing a large beaver meadow near Jackson Hole, in Wyoming. Picking my way back to the road, I came to a moderately wide but very shallow stream flowing over gravel where the deepest spots seemed incapable of holding anything but small fish. After gazing at it for a while I walked through the bushes preparatory to wading across. The minute I showed myself near the bank the entire expanse of water was covered by the tremendous thrashing of many large fish. Presumably they were trout, but they may not have been. Even very shallow water, if it's cool enough, can hold large fish. Later I wondered why these fish had been content to lie in such positions, obviously without cover of any sort. Probably the place rarely was fished, so they may have thought protection unnecessary.

On that day in the beaver meadow many large trout of several species were cruising about. It was nearing noontime and, under sunny conditions, it was very difficult to take any, even with long leaders and the smallest flies. The next morning, before sunrise, was a different story, however. On arriving at the deep, slow-flowing stream, I cast a fly to the far bank and had an immediate hit of what proved to be a three-pound rainbow. The fishing was fast and furious until the sun touched the water; then it slacked off rapidly.

On warm, sunny days it pays fishermen to get up early!

4

WHY WATER TEMPERATURES
ARE IMPORTANT

The ten percent of the fishermen who catch ninety percent of the fish seldom do it by accident. They have acquired the instinct and knowledge to go to the areas in ponds or lakes, or in rivers or small streams, where living conditions seem right for the fish they want to catch. These conditions mainly are suitable water temperature, nearness to a food supply, and protection from enemies; the latter meaning either cover or depth or both.

Of these, the most important is water temperature, which will be dealt with in this and in future chapters. For example, bass fishermen know that when the sun is high in summer the surface water is warm, and bass usually will be down deep. However, in early morning or in the evening, when surface water is cooler, bass will come into the shallows to feed. While this is a useful nugget of knowledge, there's much more to it than that!

Ideal Temperature

Every species of fish enjoys a certain water temperature wherein it is most active. In it, the fish actively cruise around in search of food and take lures readily. When the water varies higher or lower from this ideal temperature they will become less active, or they will go where temperatures are as nearly ideal as they can find. Thus, there is an ideal temperature and a tolerant range; the tolerant range perhaps affording fair fishing, but not the best. Above and below the tolerant range the fishes' metabolism (or activity) slows down so much that they have little desire to feed or to move around. If they can find more suitable temperatures, they will go where they are, just as people usually try to avoid excess cold or heat.

In the case of the popular trout and char families, for example (we'll refer to both as "trout"), we see that their ideal temperatures are between 58 and 63 degrees, and in this range they should be most active. Above and below their ideal temperatures they become increasingly sluggish and less inclined to feed. Below 48 degrees and above 68 degrees (give or take a degree or two due to regional variations) it hardly is worth fishing for them, although anglers who fish through the ice know that they will take baits occasionally if they happen to be dropped very close to them.

When streams are high and cold in the spring I have seen big brook trout lying in the grasses near the bank almost at the surface. They were so cold they wouldn't move until they were prodded to do so. In this cold water, digestive processes are so slow that fish have almost no need for food, and refuse to accept a wiggling worm even if it is drifted to their mouths. Evidently they are in these exposed places because the sun warms the surface water slightly more there. This also is a reason (and a fishing tip) why fish in lakes where the water is uncomfortably cold for them often lie in the slightly warmer, shallow water near shore.

When the air and the surface water are cold, fish may bite better around noon than early in the morning or late in the evening. Then, insect hatches occur more often around mid-day. This may be a tip for fishermen who enjoy the tradition of getting up early to go fishing on opening day in cold climates. Too many of them start at sunrise; put up with cold hands and lines freezing in line-guides, and come home later in the morning perhaps relatively fishless! Old hands at the game often sleep late on cold mornings and go fishing in the warmer hours of mid-day when the chances are better.

Ideal temperatures and the tolerant ranges are given in *Figure 9* for principal freshwater species. Don't fault the chart if local conditions vary a bit, as they may in some places. From a national standpoint they are as correct as a chart can make them.

Food Supply Important

Of course, fishermen may find many areas in any body of water where ideal temperatures exist, but that's only the first part of the decision of where to find fish. However, it's usually the most important part. Two other conditions also should apply. In the areas of the most suitable water temperatures we can find we should concentrate fishing in those places which also are near a food supply and which offer protection either of cover or depth, or both. When

TEMPERATURE-ACTIVITY TABLE
FOR FRESHWATER FISH

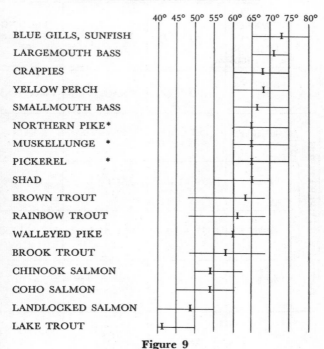

Figure 9

NOTE: "I" indicates ideal temperature. While this may vary somewhat in various regions, this chart should be followed unless regional data suggests variation. The horizontal line indicates optimum temperature range. Fish usually will not take lures well outside of this range.

* Members of the Pike family, which includes northern pike, muskellunge and the various pickerels, are much less fussy about water temperatures than other species. While the range shown for them is the optimum one, they usually will take lures when the water is slightly warmer or very much colder.

TEMPERATURE-ACTIVITY TABLE

	AT WATER SURFACE TEMPERATURES	WATER IS	FISH ARE	FISHING SHOULD BE
	FREEZING TO 40° F	MUCH TOO COLD	INACTIVE	VERY POOR
TOLERANT TEMPERATURES	40°–50° F	TOO COLD	PASSIVE	FAIR
TOLERANT TEMPERATURES; OPTIMUM TEMPERATURES	50°–60° F	JUST RIGHT	ACTIVE	GOOD
TOLERANT TEMPERATURES; OPTIMUM TEMPERATURES	60°–70° F	JUST RIGHT	VERY ACTIVE	EXCELLENT
TOLERANT TEMPERATURES	70°–80° F	TOO WARM*	ACTIVE TO PASSIVE*	FAIR
	80° F AND UP	MUCH TOO WARM	INACTIVE	VERY POOR

Figure 10

* Temperatures very close to 60° are best for Brown and for Rainbow Trout. Brook Trout enjoy water a few degrees colder. While all anglers and scientists will not agree completely with these ranges, they are the most generally accepted.

FOR TROUT

FISH ARE FOUND	SUGGESTED LURES
VERY DEEP (In lakes or pools)	BAIT FISHED DEEP
DEEP (Or along shorelines or riffles where water is warmer)	LIVE BAIT SPOONS OR SPINNERS NYMPHS STREAMER FLIES
NEAR SURFACE	WET FLIES STREAMER FLIES NYMPHS SPOONS OR SPINNERS
NEAR SURFACE	DRY OR WET FLIES STREAMER FLIES NYMPHS SPOONS OR SPINNERS
DEEP (Or in spring holes, brook mouths, shaded streams)	LIVE BAIT STREAMER FLIES NYMPHS SPOONS OR SPINNERS
VERY DEEP (Or in spring holes and cold water brooks)	BAIT FISHED DEEP

we know how or where to find such areas we can be quite sure of good fishing in them. For bass, the areas may be underwater stumps, brush piles, lily pads or ridges off grassy points. For perch, they may be weed beds on underwater reefs. For walleyes, they may be rocky points or shoals, sandbars, or stream mouths where the depth drops off sharply. We'll learn more about this as we go along.

When ideal situations are found, the trick then is to know what bait or lure to use. For this purpose *Figure 10* shows a Temperature-Activity Table for Trout. Favorite lures vary as much in various regions as do fishing methods, both according to local conditions. However, with this table as an example, it should be quite simple for fishermen to make up similar ones for their favorite species.

How do we determine ideal temperatures? From the information provided in *Figure 9,* and from a casual inspection of surface water conditions, we can make a rough guess as to where to fish, and whether we should do it on or near the surface or approximately how much deeper. This is what fishermen usually do and, while it may be better than nothing, it is not accurate enough for ideal fishing.

Fish-Finder Devices

A better way, which is easy on the pocket-book, is to obtain a "fish-finder" thermometer, or "depthometer," from a tackle store or a fishing tackle mail-order house. Attach this to a length of fishing line on which depth indications have been marked. A knot can be tied in the line for a measured length of ten feet; two close knots for twenty feet, and so on. A sinker may have to be fastened to the bottom of the thermometer to get it down quickly.

Ordinary thermometers won't do because they change readings as they are pulled up. In fish-finder thermometers the bulb is contained in a cup for water entrapment, or they may be of the shakedown type. But since even these don't record deep-water temperatures very accurately, especially on hot days, it is advisable to deduct two or three degrees from the readings obtained.

Take a surface reading and check it with *Figure 9*. If surface water is close to the ideal temperature for the kind of fishing we want to do, we can fish on or near the surface in areas that offer food and protection for fish. If surface water is too warm, lower the thermometer to the ten-foot depth; let it stay down half a minute or so, and then draw it up and read again. If we still haven't found the level of ideal temperature, take more readings at increasing five-foot depth intervals, until the right depth level is located. That is the level of productive fishing, and it should be excellent in areas at that depth near feeding spots and protection. Places like submerged weed beds and rocks often provide both.

A much more practical and low-cost instrument which records both water temperature and depth is called a Depth-O-Plug. This can be cast as a plug and allowed to sink to the bottom to locate the depth and water temperature of drop-offs, ledges, etc., as well as to read the temperatures at varying depths in a lake or pool.

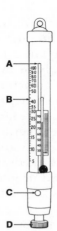

Figure 11. Depth-O-Plug tells depth and water temperature at the same time.

Figure 12. Electronic depth thermometer, the Fish-N-Temp, records depth and water temperature on scale by lowering a probe on the end of a wire.

As shown in *Figure 11,* when valve *D* is closed the water enters through the hole in the bottom of the screw and overflows at the top of the tube at *A,* where it is trapped inside the transparent barrel. As depth increases, water pressure increases, thus forcing more and more water into the barrel. Thus the depth can be read directly on the scale, such as at *B.* The barrel also contains a thermometer on which the water temperature can be read of the depth indicated. The barrel is emptied before another use by unscrewing valve *D* and shaking the water out at hole *C.* This entrapped water will roughly indicate its degree of clearness. Since one can't get everything in an instrument costing less than five dollars, it is necessary to lower, raise, and clear it for each depth reading.

Fishermen who habitually work deep-water areas often think it best to pay a higher price for an instrument which provides temperature readings quicker and easier. One of the least expensive of these is called a Fish-n-Temp. Costing in the fifty-dollar range, it is much easier on the pocketbook than the more elaborate instruments to be described later. About the bulk of a three-cell flashlight, the instrument has a temperature-reading dial where the flashlight lens would be. The body of the unit pulls open to reveal a covered fine wire 100 feet long coiled around the enclosed body. Depth measurements are printed on the covered wire at one-foot intervals. A small probe (sometimes called a sensory element or "thermistor") is attached to the wire's end and a four-ounce bell sinker is fastened to a snap near the probe. By uncoiling the wire and gradually lowering the weighted probe, the water temperature at the probe's depth can be read directly on the dial. One merely keeps lowering the probe until the battery-operated needle on the dial points to the desired temperature, and he reads the depth of that temperature on the footage markers printed on the wire. The great advantage of this device is that it does away with the tediousness of having to lower and raise a thermometer several times before obtaining the desired depth reading. It also is more accurate and, for these two reasons (plus its relative economy), it offers a very useful and quick method of determining the desired fishing depth. In addition to locating ideal fishing depth the instrument is valuable in finding underwater springs and warmer or cooler deep currents.

A somewhat more expensive Fish Flasher instrument is supplied in a small portable case containing a probe which is placed overboard but which does not descend on a wire cable. This battery-operated electronic device transmits and receives sonar sound waves at the rate of many pulsations per second. These waves are projected by the transducer into the water in a cone-shaped pattern. When they hit an object within the pattern they are reflected back to the transducer so the depth can be read on the dial as a flashing light or lights, depending on the sound waves being reflected. Thus, the instrument can tell when the boat is over or approaching individual fish or schools of fish, as well as their depth and the depth of water under the boat. Units of this sort usually are effective to

Figure 13. Flash and beeper-type electronic thermometers locate fish and tell their depth.

120 feet of depth, and under favorable conditions (such as sand, gravel, or rock bottoms), can be read to twice that depth. They are effective in salt or muddy water, as well as for fishing through the ice.

Another somewhat similar unit includes a "beeper" which can be set to sound off at any predetermined depth to locate fish or to detect underwater obstacles. Such instruments are valuable also in locating submerged reefs (which can be havens for fish) and as navigational aids.

As an example of the efficiency of these units, we were trolling live bait one day for lake trout, relaxing in the boat's stern with two lead-cored lines out. Suddenly the man running the boat called out, "We are approaching a reef at twenty-three feet depth. There are four big fish near it. Let out two more colored sections of line and you'll be trolling at the right depth. I'll bring the boat over the fish."

A minute or so later he turned and said, "The baits should be near the fish now, so be ready!" Just then there were heavy strikes on both lines, and two large lake trout were brought to net.

Thus, while these units may cost in the $100 to $200 range, or even more, they can be excellent investments for those who frequently fish large lakes or ocean areas. One should take time to investigate the various types available in order to decide which will best do the job intended, at the most acceptable price. Instead of probes, flashers, or beepers, some of the more elaborate models are equipped with rolls of paper tape on which are lines marking water depth. When the unit is turned on, a pen constantly traces a graph of the area ahead of the boat, recording water depth as well as (by small dashed lines) the locations of fish and their depths over the bottom or near reefs.

The more expensive of these devices can be rented, which is helpful to fishermen going on vacation who do not need such instruments year-round.

Fishing at Proper Depth

Of course it is one thing to know how deep we should fish and it is quite another to be sure we are fishing at the proper depth. There are several ways of knowing how much line we are pulling from the reel. We can measure the strip (conveniently, two feet) by marking a spot on the rod or measuring in relation to a rod guide. Thus, for example, ten counted strips (measured pulls) is twenty feet. Metal lines sometimes are marked at measured intervals by drops of solder; ordinary felt-tipped pens can be used to mark others, and some are provided in different colors every ten or twenty feet.

In stillfishing, such as fishing through the ice, the correct line length to reach proper depth thus is determined easily. In "mooching," that is, drifting in a boat with a weighted bait out, we should let out added line to allow for the speed of drift, or of the current. With a moderate drift or in a moderate current, perhaps twice as much line should be let out; for example, eighty feet to reach forty feet of depth. This knowledge comes from experience and there seems to be no easy rule for it except to experiment a bit until strikes indicate the bait is at the right level.

In trolling at proper depth the situation is complicated by the fact that the faster the boat is moving the nearer to the surface the bait tends to troll. Of course, the proper trolling speed is the speed which provides ideal lure action; a matter which can be determined by watching the bait while it is being trolled near the surface. Trolling depth is influenced by boat speed, which also may be influenced by wind and perhaps by current. In addition, it is influenced by the weight and amount of water resistance of the lure, by the weight of the line or by weight added to it; and perhaps by other factors. Trolling depth is discussed on pages (84) and (85). One learns mainly by experience and experiment. For example, if a lake bottom is fairly level we now know how to determine its depth. We know the speed at which the lure swims best. By trolling at that speed we can let out a measured amount of line until the lure begins to touch bottom. Knowing how much line is needed to reach that depth, it is easier to determine how much line to let out to reach a desired shallower or deeper level elsewhere with the same equipment.

Proper trolling speed therefore is very important in obtaining ideal bait action and in working the bait consistently at the proper depth. Since speed is influenced by wind and perhaps by current, it is almost impossible to estimate it with any degree of accuracy. Fortunately, low-cost speed indicators are available. Some of these consist merely of a short line with a weight attached to it and to a pointer which indicates true water speed on a simple dial affixed to the side of the boat. The greater the speed, the greater drag is put on the weight, thus pulling the pointer forward on the dial. It's as simple as that! Being sure of trolling speed is a very important part of efficient trolling.

In deep fishing, availability of food supply and of oxygen is important, but the necessity for cover (or protection) decreases as the cruising depth of fish increases. The ideal depth will apply everywhere in the lake except possibly where there are underwater springs or incoming streams.

When taking water temperature readings by lowering a thermometer to increasing depths in summer, fishermen who are beginners at the game may be surprised to find that the temperature drops suddenly and very sharply at a certain depth, and that this is true for about this depth everywhere in the lake. This level of rapid temperature change is called the "thermocline," and it often is considered to be the level of good fishing. This phenomenon is so important to successful lake and large pond fishing that it deserves a section of its own, so we'll learn more about it in Chapter 6.

5

WHERE TO FIND FISH IN PONDS

Ponds differ widely in what they offer to fish, but the various species of fish do not vary in what they need in them. Perhaps ponds can be classified very roughly as cold-water ones such as are found in northern regions and warm-water ponds mostly located in the South, although here and there and in between are cool-water ones which have some of the characteristics of both. Knowledgeable fishermen who suddenly find themselves anywhere in North America can make surprisingly accurate guesses not only as to the species a given pond should contain, but also where in the pond the hotspots are which should offer the best fishing. But no matter how experienced an angler is in his ability to "read the water," he is much better off with a local fisherman to guide him. Every region seems to have its own ground rules in lures and where and how to fish them. Local tricks of the trade often are unusual, and they invariably get the best results.

Cold-Water Ponds

In New England we have cold-water ponds which often contain Eastern brook trout. If their temperatures in summer go much higher than 65 degrees they contain cold-water springs or are fed by cold-water brooks where the fish go in warm weather to cool off.

One of these is Quimby's Pond, in Maine—a famous natural brook-trout pond where the fishing remains fairly good (occasionally very good) in spite of the great numbers of anglers who fish it. Part of the reason for this is the dense weed beds on its shallow, spring-fed bottom which offer an ideal combination of protection and food. The other part is because artificial flies only are allowed. This is a very sensible rule of Maine's very efficient Fish and Game Department which has prevented the pond from becoming fished out even though it never has been stocked. Fishing usually is from boats. Motors are not permitted.

At first glance even a capable water reader would see no characteristics to go on because the pond's bottom is flat and relatively shallow, with no hotspots visible from the surface; not even an entering brook of any importance. If there are open spaces between the weed beds, they are not obvious. Many cold-water ponds are the same.

The trick here is to anchor in almost any spot and to cast a long sinking line as far as can be done without excessive effort, probably using a small bucktail or streamer fly fished moderately fast, or a nymph or a well-trimmed wet fly fished *very* slowly. Allow the fly and line to sink for a minute or two before retrieving. If the fly doesn't pick up weeds occasionally, it may not be going deep enough. If one has no strikes after fanwise casting in various directions he pulls anchor and tries another place. When a trout is hooked the angler casts to the same spot again. If another one is caught there, the hotspot may

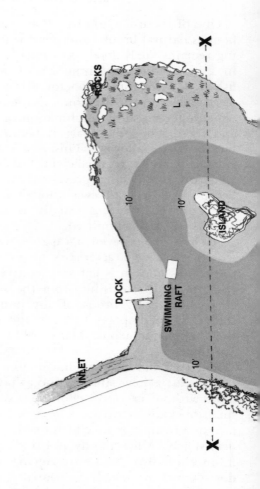

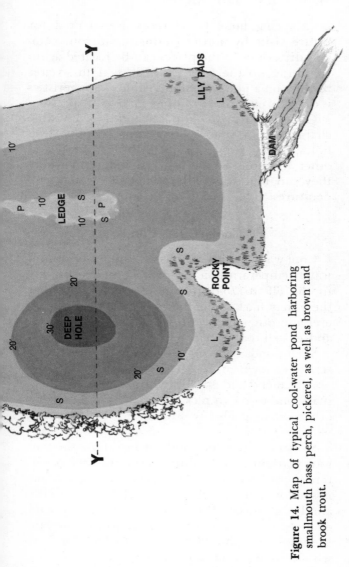

Figure 14. Map of typical cool-water pond harboring smallmouth bass, perch, pickerel, as well as brown and brook trout.

be a spring hole. Good spots are marked for future visits by noting landmarks in four compass directions so the places can be located again by lining up the four landmarks. Thus, water reading on a pond without visible characteristics is done by experiment rather than by inspection.

Of course, many cold-water ponds have visible characteristics such as entering brooks, deep holes, rocky ledges or reefs, brush piles, and other locations where fish can hide and where they can find seasonally acceptable water temperatures. This makes it easier.

Cool-Water Ponds

Cool-water ponds may have summer optimum water temperatures a few degrees higher, usually in the 60- to 75-degree range. We know that these may harbor smallmouth bass, perch, pickerel and other pond fish, as well as brown trout and even brook trout.

Such ponds have some or many of the characteristics shown in *Figure 14,* so let's start at the northern end and go clockwise around this imaginary one to try to pick the good locations from others that probably aren't worth bothering with.

Starting at the dock and rowing along the ten-foot contour line nothing seems worthy of interest until we reach the cove where the water is shallow and sprinkled with clumps of weeds amid the rocks. When surface water is cool enough, or in summer's early mornings or late evenings, this should be a good place for bass which come from the deeper water into the shallows to feed. (Between the ten-foot contour

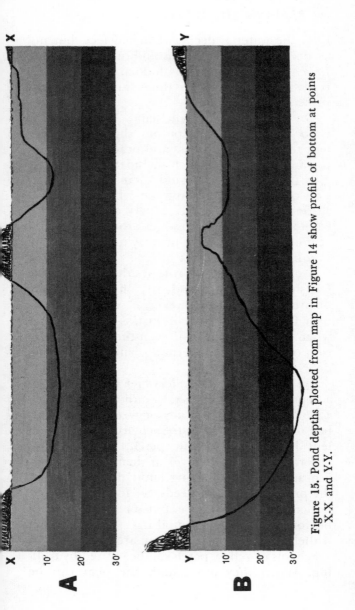

Figure 15. Pond depths plotted from map in Figure 14 show profile of bottom at points X-X and Y-Y.

lines the water is deeper than ten feet, but not as deep as twenty feet as indicated in *Figure 15 A*.) Pickerel should be hidden in the grasses, ready to rush out to hit almost any lure or bait presented to them.

On the right is a small island. If its shoreline is rocky, the ten-foot contour should be excellent for smallmouth bass and other members of the Sunfish family, which includes sunfish, blue-gills (bream), crappies and their kin. The best side of the island should be where it casts a shadow on the water. It is very convenient for fish to lie in the deeper water around the island at midday and to travel in early morning or late evening to the shallows to feed.

From this point we row south, ignoring the left shore because it evidently offers no feeding or protective areas. However, if surface water is near freezing, fish may lie in this shallow water when the sun warms it if even the slight protection of small rocks, overhung banks, or floating debris is available.

On the right is an underwater ledge rising to a depth of about five feet, as indicated in *Figure 15 B*. If the ledge is rocky or weedy it can harbor many species of fish. Such ledges are excellent habitats for yellow perch, and bass and other gamefish will travel to them seeking baitfish and other food lying amid the rocks or in the protection of the weeds. Such ledges may be noticed from the surface, but some may need to be found by taking soundings. This is worth while because invariably they are hotspots.

Schools of yellow perch can be located by trolling. When they are found, the boat can be anchored because the school may not leave the area. A favorite method is to let baits sink naturally, using worms, minnows, and other types, or even a piece of a worm, if the fish are small. Baits which sink slowly and naturally are much more effective than quick sinkers carrying too much lead.

Farther along, on the southeast edge of the pond, is another shallow area which is sandy rather than rocky and which has large patches of lily pads here and there mixed with weeds. If a pond is nearly covered with pads, all of it should be productive, but lily-pad areas, large or small, are hotspots for most species of pond fish, especially bass and pickerel. One may need to use weedless lures, casting on to pads rimming a patch of open water and then pulling the lure from the pad into the water.

Now we come to the pond's outlet which, in this case, is a small dam. Presumably the gradually shelving gravel bottom affords a minimum of food and protection, so we'll pass it by unless we see something that invites investigation.

Another hotspot is the rocky point with grasses extending into fairly deep water. Such points don't need to be rocky to be hotspots because members of the Sunfish family should be lying beside the ridge and off its point at a depth of several feet or more. Let's anchor so we can cast to the deep water off the point, gradually extending the casts to cover the entire area. One of the author's favorite methods for such places is to use a weighted weedless plastic worm. Let it sink to the bottom and fish it in extremely slowly with slight twitches so it appears to be crawling along the bottom. If protection is offered in the coves on each side of the point, these also should be good places.

While we are fishing around this point let's observe an important tip in water reading. The point points to the island, and we know there is a ledge in between. If we don't know the ledge is there, we can assume it may be because the geological situation offered by the point and the island would indicate that an underwater ridge could extend in between. In this case this opinion could be more valid because we note a very steep bank on the western side of the pond. A steep bank extending into the water may indicate greater depth there, especially if the steep bank is composed of rock. Thus, if we didn't have the map to go by, we could make an estimate of the probable situation and assume that all of these characteristics exist.

The steep bank on the western shore is a hotspot because it is heavily wooded and rocky, offering deep-water protection, shade in the afternoon, and an obvious food supply provided by the trees, undergrowth, and rocks. If we took depth readings here we would find an underwater contour resembling *Figure 15 B*. If surface water is warm, gamefish would move to this deep hole during the day and would travel to the ledge or to the other feeding areas we have noticed when cooler surface waters exist in early morning or late evening.

Finally, before we return to the dock, we check the entering brook at the inlet. If surface water is warm, fish may be in this cooler water. If the inlet drops off steeply as it enters the pond, this drop-off would be a hotspot—especially for trout, if any should be in residence.

On returning to the dock we might try a few casts around the swimming raft lying off the dock, if the area hasn't recently been disturbed by people and boats. Bass like to lie in the shade of rafts and docks, and these all offer good fishing locations. If surface water is warm, the bass may not be there, but such places always are congregating spots for smaller fish such as bluegills and sunfish. Tiny baits or lures on very light tackle provide good sport at any time of day and, while the fillets of these fish are small, they are easy to prepare, delicious when dipped in seasoned flour or crumbs and fried lightly to a golden brown in the skillet.

Warm-Water Ponds

The third type is warm-water ponds which, because they are located in southern regions, do not usually freeze over in the winter and maintain fairly constant temperatures year-round. They may be connected to larger lakes by waterways, and are like many of the southern lakes except in size. These are the habitats of the various basses and their cousins, the crappies, bluegills (bream) and their kin. Crappies, somewhat unlike the basses, are pool and lake fish which dislike currents, weed beds, and rush-infested areas. They prefer the substantial protection of sunken brush piles, submerged logs, wharfs, and rock bars, but they occasionally frequent isolated patches of pads and weeds growing on a sandy bottom. The big ones usually are taken in deep water.

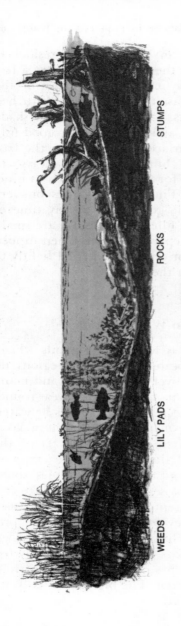

WEEDS   LILY PADS   ROCKS   STUMPS

Figure 16. Underwater view of a typical warm-water pond holding bass and panfish.

Some ponds (and lakes) in the South are shallow and grassy; others are deep and sprinkled with stumps, cypress knees, and brush. All these areas are havens for fish.

Beaver Ponds

In northern regions beavers dam streams or the outlets of ponds to provide expanses of water large enough for gathering their food supply of green tree trunks and branches which they fell and cut up by gnawing with their teeth and tow to the food area where they are sunk for winter use. Beaver ponds may or may not provide good fishing (usually for trout), depending on their age.

When the pond is new, trout which previously inhabited the feeder brook multiply and grow fat on insect life and other food newly accessible to them due to the greater expanse of the pond's surface, which now submerges the low areas of the green shoreline. Good fishing may last for a short period of years, but then something happens to spoil it.

As the submerged green vegetation dies it no longer gives off oxygen and no longer encourages insect and aquatic life. The dying trees, bushes, and grasses rot and give off carbon dioxide, thus depriving the pond of oxygen and making it unsuitable for fish. One can "read" this condition by observing bubbles of gas rising to the surface. Without oxygen, we have noticed that fish cannot exist, so the pond becomes dead from a fishing standpoint. Such ponds often are devoid of any noticeable life whatsoever.

After a few years of this dormant condition, if the dam still exists to preserve the water level, a period of rejuvenation sets in. So much of the former growth has completely rotted that the carbon dioxide content of the pond has been reduced to a minimum. Grasses, pads, and rushes start to grow in the fertile muck, thus gradually returning the balance of oxygen again, a balance which also is stimulated by wave action, which provides dissolved oxygen from the air. Fish in the feeder brooks slowly return to the pond, and insect and aquatic life begins to exist once more. The renewed pond again may contain trout, but the change in its ecology may make it more suitable for bass, pickerel and other pond fish. This would depend, as we have seen, upon the temperature of the new pond and what species of fish have been able to return to it.

One of the points that has been stressed is that fish require adequate dissolved oxygen in water in order for them to exist in it. Beaver ponds are good examples of this. The quality of the fishing in them depends largely on how much oxygen they contain.

6

WHY LAKES TURN OVER

In northern regions the news that "The ice is out!" signals quick packing and a fast trip to anglers' chosen lakes because traditionally the week or two immediately following the breaking up of the ice is a period of excellent fishing. Although this is true to a large extent, temperature conditions may exist which would recommend making the trip a bit later. The occurrence points to the necessity of understanding the behavior of northern lakes because this proven pattern of behavior has a profound influence on fishing during the many months of open water.

One day the surfaces of lakes are great expanses of ice which have gradually thinned and become porous and rotten due to the increasing heat of the sun as spring advances. The next day, seemingly without warning, the ice has disappeared and the clear, cold water often dimples and boils with the rises and rollings of fish newly freed from their winter-long imprisonment in the coldness of the depths.

Why is one of the best fishing times just after the ice goes out? Why don't lakes freeze from top to bottom, or nearly so? Why is fishing poor near the surface in summer? If we want to troll, how deep should we fish for best results?

These questions, and many others, are answered by knowledge of the seasonal changes peculiar to cold-water lakes, which is part of the science of limnology. It pays rich dividends when anglers understand what happens, and why.

Winter Stagnation

The nub of what happens revolves around the fact that water is heaviest (of greatest density) when it is at a temperature of 39.2 degrees F. When it is colder or warmer than 39.2 degrees the water is lighter, and thus tends to rise to the surface, displacing the heavier water and causing it to sink to the bottom.

The winter stagnation period is shown in *Figure 17*. An insulating blanket of ice covers the lake, with the water just below it slightly above the freezing temperature of 32 degrees. Below this, the water becomes gradually warmer (and heavier) until the temperature of maximum density of 39.2 degrees is reached at the bottom. The presence of this relatively warmer water explains why lakes don't freeze solid in winter.

Plants which live in water provide food for baitfish, which in turn provide food for larger fish. But water plants need sunlight, which helps them to absorb carbon dioxide and to give off oxygen, in order to grow. There is a depth in deep lakes below which sufficient sunlight does not penetrate. This depth depends on the degree of clarity of the water. Since at and below this depth there is insufficient plant life and oxygen, very few fish will be found there.

These facts provide tips on where to fish through the ice. We know that, in very cold water, fish seek the warmest temperatures they

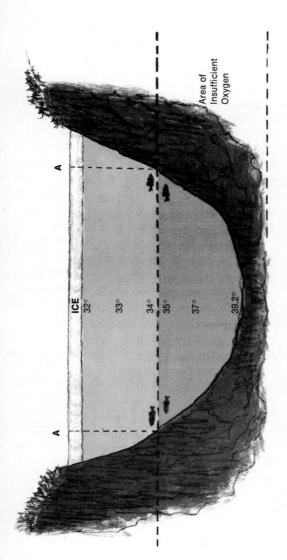

Figure 17. Winter stagnation period of a northern lake. Under layer of ice, water becomes increasingly warmer at lower depths, reaching 39.2 F on the bottom.

can find where there also is plant life to provide food. These two conditions are met at the greatest depth where there is sufficient oxygen along the shoreline, so we should cut our ice-fishing holes at the two positions marked *A*. Since this depth varies from lake to lake, we have to locate it by trial and error, but it helps to explain why some fishing holes are productive while others are not. A sounding can be taken of the depth of a productive hole, and other holes should be bored where the lake's bottom contour is at this depth. If a hole is bored where the depth is much more or less than the productive depth, a better hole can be cut nearer or farther from shore.

Hotspots for ice fishing are found where reefs rise from the lake bottom into a level of sufficient oxygen. They are found where underground springs pour relatively warmer water into the lake.

Spring Turnover

When the ice breaks up the spring turnover stage begins, as shown in *Figure 18*. This happens when the increasing warmth of early spring raises the water surface temperature from near-freezing to 39.2 degrees. At this time all the water in the lake is of approximately equal (and maximum) density. A wind blowing on the lake therefore can push the surface water and cause it to mix with the deeper water, thus actually causing all the water in the lake to "turn over."

When this condition happens, making all the water of the same temperature, fish which have been in the depths come to the surface and feed ravenously to make up for their period of semi-starvation during the winter. Should we, therefore, fish anywhere on the surface? Some places are much better than others.

The wind blowing across the surface of the lake (as shown in *Figure 18*) is blowing surface food to the eastern shore, so this shoreline should be most productive. But the surface water, at not much over 39.2 degrees, still is too cold for most species of fish to enjoy. They therefore try to rest and to feed where it is warmer. This is in shallow areas where the sun has warmed the surface water to a greater degree than it has in deeper areas of the lake.

In early spring, for this reason, we find fish very close to the shoreline, perhaps lying in water too shallow for boats. The trick is to run the boat very slowly within casting distance from the shoreline and to cast very close to shore, preferably to the shore toward which the breeze is blowing. Large fish, such as trout and land-locked salmon, may (and probably will) be lying in water almost too shallow to float them!

Finally, we should add a word of warning to anglers who want to rush to their favorite fishing lake on the day that the ice is out. Ice goes out partly due to wind action. If this wind action has been insufficient, the waters in the lake may not have mixed, and the majority of fish may not have come to the surface. It is handy to have a friend at the lake who can take temperature readings and who can tell you when surface temperatures have reached 40 degrees or so and also, perhaps, that the fish are biting. Depend-

Figure 18. During spring turnover period, surface water warms to 39.2. Wind mixes water, causing lake to "turn over." Fish in the depths then rise to the surface and feed hungrily.

ing on how windy and how warm it is, the ideal time for early fishing may be a week or two after the ice has left. The ideal time usually lasts for two or three weeks, or possibly more, until warmer weather raises surface temperatures and causes the lake to stratify. The spring turnover stage and the fall turnover stage (both of which are very similar) are the two times when cold-water fish such as lake trout and landlocked salmon can be caught on the surface.

Summer Stratification

As spring progresses into summer, the surface water becomes increasingly warmer. Since it is warmer, and thus lighter than the water below, it stays on top. This warm surface water reaches down to meet the colder water below at a depth of twenty feet or so, or perhaps much more; this depth depending on the size of the lake and various weather conditions. Where the warm top layer meets the cold bottom layer, a certain amount of mixing takes place thus making a third intermediate layer which is a layer of rapid drop in temperature. This middle layer may be between twenty and forty feet thick, again depending on lake size and weather conditions. In any lake this intermediate layer remains quite constant all summer long. It is called the "thermocline," and it is the level of good fishing.

Scientists call the top layer the "epilimnion" and the bottom layer the "hypolimnion," but these words are tonguetwisters and we don't need to bother with them.

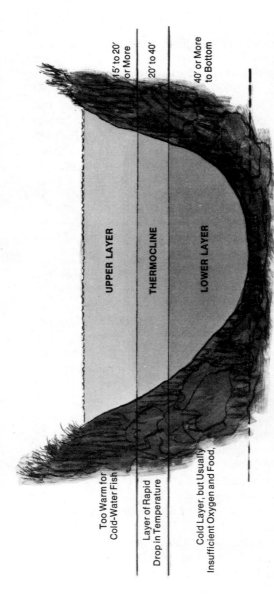

Figure 19. Lake stratifies during summer into three layers. Best fishing is in the thermocline near sides of lake or at that depth around islands and submerged reefs.

UPPER LAYER

THERMOCLINE

LOWER LAYER

15' to 20' or More

20' to 40'

40' or More to Bottom

Too Warm for Cold-Water Fish

Layer of Rapid Drop in Temperature

Cold Layer, but Usually Insufficient Oxygen and Food,

In choosing where they will spend the summer, cold-water fish dislike the lower layer of the lake because we have seen that it usually contains insufficient oxygen and plant life, and therefore insufficient food. They dislike the upper layer because it is too warm. Thus they cruise in or very near to the thermocline level. In staying at this level they also want to be near protection and food, which means they usually will be found where this level meets the sides of the lake, or at this depth around islands and submerged reefs. They may leave this level to come nearer the surface where cold-water streams enter the lake and, under certain conditions, they may come into the shallows of warmer water in the evening or during the night to feed. However, in summer, the thermocline level is our best bet (*Figure 19*).

We have seen that we can find the thermocline level by taking readings at increasing depths with a water thermometer of one type or another. For the first twenty feet or so readings at five-foot intervals will be very much the same. Then, suddenly the instrument will indicate a rapid drop in temperature. This colder water will become rapidly still colder as increasingly deeper readings are taken, and then the readings will level off when the instrument is dropped below the thermocline level. (The thermocline, technically, is the layer where the drop in temperature is at least one degree Centigrade per meter of depth.)

Thus, for the best summer fishing we should stillfish or troll at the thermocline level where

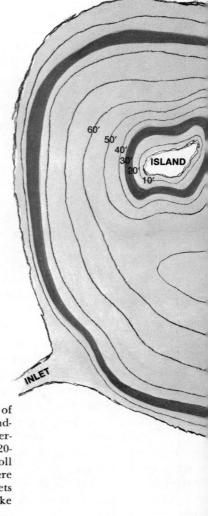

60'
50'
40'
30'
20'
10'
ISLAND

INLET

Figure 20. The paths of good trolling. Soundings indicate the thermocline is at the 20- to 30-foot depth. Troll at this depth where the thermocline meets the sides of the lake and of the island.

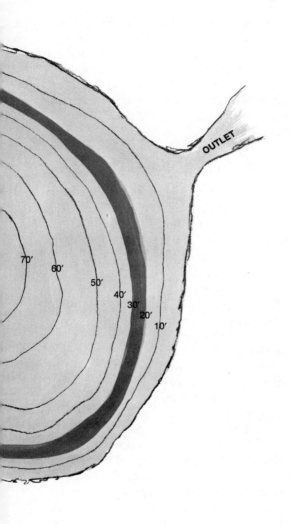

this level is near the land. If we can obtain a contour map of the lake (or want to bother to make one) we can chart the path of good trolling which, in simplified form, might look something like *Figure 20*. We know the optimum temperature choices of the kinds of fish we want to catch (*page* 47) and we should consider these in making decisions.

Trolling at Proper Depth

Of course it is one thing to know how deep to troll and it is another problem to know whether or not our lures are being trolled at that proper depth. The trolling depth is decided by the amount of line put out; the weight of the line, and the speed of the boat—plus lead we have added, if any.

A fellow angler who usually is very successful has solved the problem in this way, and many others do it similarly. He uses a low-cost fiberglass flyrod about $8\frac{1}{2}$ feet long and a large and sturdy fly reel containing two or three hundred feet of fine monel wire line. The forward part of the line is marked every twenty-five feet (so, for example, four marks indicate he has a hundred feet of wire line out). Swiveled to the end of the wire is at least fifty feet (or as much as a hundred feet) of twenty-pound test monofilament. To the end of this is tied about ten feet of ten-pound monofilament, with the lure attached to this. He knows about how much wire line to let out for the depth he wants to fish, and he has a speed indicator on his outboard-powered boat to insure trolling at the correct and steady speed, which, of course, is influenced by the force and direction of the wind. If the amount of line out doesn't result in strikes, he takes in or lets out some until he gets results. Then he trolls with that measured amount of line out, at that speed, until he has reason to change. When a fish is hooked he can reel in the wire line and can play the fish on the monofilament, as one would do in fly fishing. If the lure becomes caught on the bottom and can't be freed, the light ten-pound tippet breaks, thus saving his long length of twenty-pound-test terminal line. He previously had determined the thermocline depth and he knows he is fishing at that depth when he has the predetermined amount of line out and is trolling at the proper speed.

Although he knows that he is trolling at the proper depth, just below, in, or above the thermocline, there still may be the question of whether or not his trolling path is bringing the lure close enough to the shore of the lake. He may guide the boat nearer shore until he touches bottom or grasses, then troll a bit farther out. The method is relatively simple, once one gets used to it, and it is an excellent way to enjoy good fishing.

Fall Turnover

Finally fall arrives, and cold nights lower surface-water temperatures until the reverse of the spring turnover stage (*Figure 18*) takes place. When the surface water has cooled to 39.2 degrees, all the water in the lake is of such similar density that wind action can mix it and equalize it at 39.2 degrees. Since the thermocline and the warm upper layer then no longer exist, the fish which have been living at thermocline level, or near it, now come to the surface again and can be caught on top. Cold-water fish, such as lake trout, coho and landlocked salmon, provide top sport with surface lures around islands, reefs, and shorelines. The fall turnover period lasts until ice begins to form.

When the ice begins to form the winter stagnation period (*Figure 17*) sets in and the annual cyclic behavior of northern lakes is completed.

Lake Trout

Thus, if we want to fish for very cold-water species such as lake trout, the best times to do it for greatest sport are during the weeks in the spring and in the fall when no thermal stratification exists and they can be caught on or near the surface. At such times they are much sportier and more lively than during summer or winter periods, when they have to be brought up from the depths and feel, at the end of a line, as someone said, "Like hauling in an old boot."

Lake trout are members of the char family (as are brook trout and Dolly Varden trout) and are referred to by various names such as "togue" in the east, "Mackinaw trout" in the west, and "gray trout" in Canada. They basically are gray-backed, with whiter spots and dark markings, and are distinguished by forked tails. Their favorite water temperature in most regions is slightly over 40 degrees, so they are at their best when lakes "turn over."

Lake trout breed in the fall and early winter (usually between September and December) over gravel or rocky bottoms near the surface in shallow lakes and as deep as a hundred feet or more in others. Thus, fall surface fishing is good over rocky ledges where they then are inclined to congregate.

In both fall and spring anglers find them in such places as well as in coves and along shorelines. In southern regions they largely are restricted to lakes having thermal stratification and with adequate dissolved oxygen in the deeper parts. When near the surface they can be caught with streamer flies or bucktails, or with spinning lures of various sorts. When deeper, one trolls for them with spoons and other hardware or with rigged bait.

As we go along in this little book we realize that "reading the water" properly includes knowing the types of locations preferred by the kinds of fish we want to catch and fishing for them in such places where the water temperatures exist which they prefer. Like people, fish can't always enjoy ideal living conditions but, like people, they do the best they can. If we know how to read the water for the fish we want to catch, we have taken the major step toward success in catching them!

7

FISHING COLD-WATER LAKES

When a pond should be termed a lake, or a small lake should be classed as a pond, often results from the whim of whomever named it, because large ponds and small lakes have very much in common. Therefore, the comments on reading the waters of ponds (as given in Chapter 5) apply to many lakes as well; especially to the pondlike bays of large lakes which, in essence, are ponds connected to the lakes by small necks of water.

What has been said in Chapters 5 and 6 should provide helpful water-reading information for most cold-water lakes, but the big ones have other things going for them.

One is the migrations of gamefish such as the various species of trout and of landlocked salmon as they pursue the spawning excursions of baitfish such as smelt and kokanee salmon. (Smelt spawn in spring; kokanee in fall and winter. Both species spawn in streams and kokanee also on the gravel shoals of lakes.) After ice leaves the lakes the smelt, in vast hoards, travel from the lakes up tributary streams and brooks to spawn. Their tiny brownish eggs often are so thickly encrusted on rocks and roots as to completely cover them. With this mission accomplished, the smelt return to the lakes.

Therefore, in lakes and reservoirs containing baitfish such as smelt, anglers should be on hand at the end of the spawning period. Big trout, landlocked salmon, and other gamefish know that feasts of smelt will be coming from the streams into the lakes, and they mass around the inlets to consume them. Thus, fishing in lakes near their inlets usually is excellent while the spawning run is going on.

Excellent? During the "hot" week or two, if we are smart and lucky enough to be there, it can be a bonanza; a fishing spree impossible at any other time of year. On a big lake in Maine, for example, a river enters which accommodates a large run of smelt. A group of anglers have a fishing camp there and can fish with flyrods and flies in a deep hole in the inlet only a moderate cast from shore. Five-pound brook trout and landlocked salmon, or even bigger, now are rare in Maine lakes, but they often are taken, along with many very respectable smaller ones, on the surface during the spring exodus of smelt from the stream. I always try to go up at the proper time but, in the last year or two, have been a few days too late for the best of the fishing. I am more or less convinced that this is the place where the familiar comment "You should have been here last Tuesday" originated!

Fishing Inlets

Anglers fishing stream mouths often fish too close in. The tendency is to consider the visible part of the outlet (*line A-A in Figure 21*) as being the important part, thus resulting, if they are fishing from a boat, in operating over the fish and putting them down. The part well out from the stream mouth usually is the important one (B-B). Often, just out from the visible part, there is a decided drop-off carved out by pre-

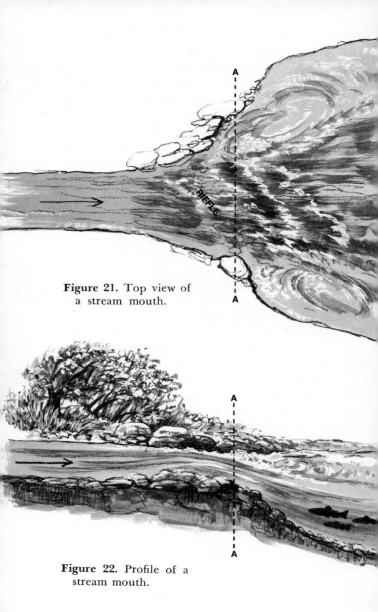

Figure 21. Top view of a stream mouth.

RIFFLE

Figure 22. Profile of a stream mouth.

vious high water. The drop-off may be steep or fairly shallow, but it will be where most of the fish lie because the slower current down deep provides a better resting place than does the more rapid flow closer in. Trout, landlocked salmon, and other species usually will be in the deeper part of the drop-off. It also is an excellent spot for walleyes, if they are in residence.

When reading the water of an inlet stream it also is useful to remember that the stream may cut a channel out into the lake; particularly if the lake has been raised by a dam. Sometimes there are channels and often there are not. If they exist, it is easy to spot them from the air or by taking soundings and to draw a sketch of the location, which may extend straight out or to the left, or nearer the southern shore (*as in Figure 23*). These channels may be surprisingly

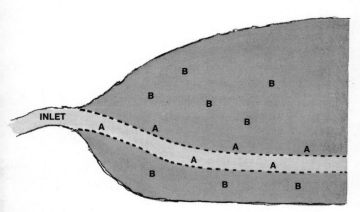

Figure 23. Try to locate the channel of an inlet stream. *A* indicates path of good fishing; *B*, poorer fishing.

deep. Fishing should be much better in the channel (in locations marked *A* in *Figure 23*) than in other parts of the inlet (as marked *B*).

Follow the Baitfish

After the smelt or other baitfish leave the streams they travel in schools, often along one shore or the other. If one can locate a school he will find that gamefish are following it. If he knows where the school is at the end of the fishing day, and in what direction it is moving, he can plot its probable position the next day, and can pin it down more accurately by trolling. Thus, over a period of several days, anglers fishing lakes after spawning runs often can catch gamefish which follow the runs. If a school becomes lost, another one probably can be located.

Local fishermen know more about the habits of migrating fish than visitors usually do. If one sees a collection of boats in any place he can surmise that they are there for a reason so, without moving in too closely, we can let others help to locate the fish for us!

Narrows

Narrows usually are hotspots, especially when fish are moving in spring and fall. These are of two basic types.

One is when two points of land divide a lake nearly into two parts, to provide sort of an hourglass effect. In traveling from one part of the lake to the other, fish must pass through the narrow section; their path, thus being confined, makes them more accessible to anglers. One can troll the narrow part at the depth that water temperatures indicate or, when surface waters are cold, he can anchor or drift in the narrows, and do his casting near the surface.

A time when fishing the narrows may not be good is when they are relatively shallow and when the lake's thermocline is deeper in the summer. Then, the warmer water in the narrows may more or less seal them off, confining game-fish in one section or the other.

Another type is a waterway between two lakes, sort of a short river with little or no flow. (In New England we call them "thorofares.") In spring and summer fish use the waterways for travel, and large fish also may wait in them for migrating baitfish, or may take up holding positions near the outlets. For these reasons, sporting camps often are built on such waterways because fishermen who stay in them may not need to travel very far to enjoy good fishing.

Spawning Migrations

Another situation is the migrations of game-fish for their own spawning. Rainbow trout spawn in the spring; brown trout and Eastern brook trout in the fall. Steelhead and Atlantic salmon have late spring, summer, and fall runs which vary from river to river. Trout other than steelhead (an anadromous rainbow trout) also go to salt water and return to the rivers periodically, so smart anglers wherever they are take the trouble to find out what's going on.

In the early spring of a year long ago, I was on Cape Cod, but dismissed thoughts of going fishing because the season seemed too early.

"Too early!" a bait-shop proprietor scoffed when I made the remark. "Go get a flyrod and a spinning rod and come with me. I'll show you something!"

He drove to a marsh through which flowed a narrow but deep tidal stream. "Cast downstream and work in the lure close to the bank," he said.

A splashing swirl rewarded the second or third cast, and I landed a fat, silvery brown trout of about three pounds, freshly in from the bay. We took several more in rapid succession and enjoyed an excellent fishing day. The season is short, however.

Trout which migrate to salt water (and sometimes up rivers from big lakes) are called "coasters" when they return to the streams. The term evidently originally was applied to brook trout descending from tributary streams to live in Lake Superior, returning in the fall fattened to weights of from three to five pounds, or more.

A knowledge of the migratory habits of game-fish helps anglers who fish big lakes at the proper times to hit paydirt. New Englanders know, for example, that brook trout and landlocked salmon leave the lakes for the streams on spawning runs in the fall. Late in the fishing season they concentrate near stream mouths prior to running up-river.

Watch for Spring Holes

In warm weather when lakes are stratified it pays to watch for spring holes, even to cruising big lakes for the express purpose of finding them. Some, as have been noted, are located by unusually lush growth on the shore, with cold water trickling down the wet bank. Others are harder to find because they are submerged, but local anglers usually know where they are. Sometimes this information is closely guarded, because local anglers know that spring holes quickly can become fished out. The overfishing of spring holes is not confined to vacationists. Too often the local people do the damage!

One year we spent the last two weeks of September on a big trout lake in Maine. An old gentleman staying at the camp used to disappear every day, returning each night, fishless. On his last evening there he brought home two beautiful large brook trout. After dinner we had a chat on the porch.

"You are an angling author," he said, "who has the reputation of fishing for fun and for rarely killing a trout. If you will go alone to the place I've been going to, and if you'll use judgment in keeping it confidential, I'll tell you where it is."

On my assurance that his secret would be protected, he directed me to a lily-pad-infested cove of the lake. "There's an open spot in the middle," he said. "It's a good spring hole. I just don't want any fish-hogs to find it and fish it out."

On locating the place the next day I observed that few anglers would bother with the cove, except perhaps for bass or pickerel. Certanly not for trout! But my sunken fly took several big brook trout in the big open circle between the pads and, in thankfulness for the old gentleman's generous advice, I released every one. I never

learned how he found the place, but evidently
he had an inquiring mind.

Cold-water lakes also include cool-water lakes,
whose temperatures are more favorable to cool-
water fish such as smallmouth bass and walleyes
than to cold-water fish such as trout and landlocked salmon. Cool-water lakes are the "in
between ones," and harbor fish such as are found
in warm water lakes, as well.

Smallmouth Bass

In Chapter 5 some of the "hotspots" for smallmouth bass in ponds were discussed. When
similar places can be found in large lakes they
should be hotspots, but in large lakes there also
are others.

Look for bronzebacks in clear, rocky lakes
which provide summer temperatures of between
60 and 75 degrees. (In southern states the bass
may be acclimated to waters about 5 degrees
warmer.) Favorite spots are where rocky banks
shelve off steeply into clear water from 10 to 20
feet deep, especially when rocks, sunken logs,
or weed beds provide protection on the bottom.
Gravel bars between weed beds are likely places,
as well as gravel points extending out from
shore. The edges of reefs in large lakes, and
underwater brushy patches, also should be good.
As noted previously, bass usually leave these
areas in the late afternoon to come to shallow
grassy or lily-padded shorelines to feed, returning to the deep holes when the morning sun
starts to warm surface waters again.

The knowledge of reading the water is helped
by knowledge of the habits of fish. Bronzebacks

spawn in the spring (between late April and early June, depending somewhat on regional conditions) when water temperatures are between 60 and 70 degrees. They build nests in sand or light gravel in water between three feet and twenty feet deep; usually, the clearer the water, the deeper the nest. Nests are easily spotted from boats because circular areas have been cleared into small depressions looking vaguely like automobile tires in the water. The male forces a selected, ripe female into the nest and sends her on her way after her eggs are laid. Then he finds another; as many as three or four, and he alone guards the nest. He is easy prey to any sort of lure because he will attack anything he thinks may bother the nest. Fishermen who cast to bass nests might remember that it is no accomplishment to catch bass on them, and that it is better conservation to leave the male fish alone to finish his job in the nursery.

Walleyes

Another great favorite of cool-water lakes is the walleyed pike, which is improperly named because he does not belong to the Pike family. His range now covers nearly all of the United States, and he is found more often in larger lakes and rivers than in smaller ones.

Walleyes are school fish which usually congregate deep in lakes or on the bottoms of rivers. We have noticed that the drop-off of an entering stream into a lake is a favorite spot to find them. They feed on shoals and sandbars near the deeper water and do it most actively in the evening and at night.

Their spawning period starts soon after the ice breaks up in spring when the water has reached temperatures in the 45- to 50-degree range. Favorite spawning spots are graveled shoal areas of the lake where there is flowing water or wave action.

Fishing the big lakes can be frustrating, even to highly experienced anglers, but the ones who are most consistently successful are those who have learned by experience, and by reading, how to determine where and how deep their favorite fish are. Knowing these basic principles makes it quicker and easier to catch them.

A brief description of a successful fishing trip several years ago to Idaho and Oregon may illustrate this. My partner was Joe Brooks, internationally famous as an angler, and currently Fishing Editor of *Outdoor Life* magazine. Joe wanted to catch a record striped bass on a flyrod, while my aim was at a record Kamloops (rainbow) trout from Idaho's Lake Pend Oreille. Both of us got our fish and, although the former wasn't caught in a lake, it helps to illustrate the point.

We arrived at Oregon's Coos Bay late at night; chartered a boat, and Joe started fishing early the next morning in the rain. After cruising around a bit and turning down several hotspots suggested by the skipper, Joe noticed a breakwater of tremendous rocks and told the boat handler to steer slowly along it at a distance of a hundred feet.

Not realizing who he had aboard, the skipper demurred. "No bass there," he said. "If you guys want to catch 'em, let me take you to the right places."

"I only want one bass—a big one," Joe replied. "Steer along the breakwater."

This was Joe's day, and I watched him with fascination as his strong arm shot powerful, long casts which dropped the little popping bug within inches of the rocks. After twitching it a bit he would pick it up and cast again.

Suddenly there was a gigantic splash as a tremendous striped bass erupted and slammed the little lure high into the air. When it dropped to the surface, he took it solidly.

Several long runs later, and after periods of sulking when Joe had to strum the tight line on a dangerously bent rod, the big bass was brought to boat. It weighed twenty-nine pounds and six ounces, and was the flyrod world record for the species.

Just to show this was no fluke, he hooked another of similar size later, but the hook wasn't embedded solidly, and it pulled out after a few minutes of action. Anyway, we had had enough for the morning.

Even years later I still marvel at Joe's instinctive ability to immediately and correctly read the water of a place he had never before visited. Ignoring the recommended spots with only casual glances, his many years of angling for the "big ones" told him exactly where he should find them.

"Your day will come," he said to me. "Wait 'till we get to Pend Oreille!"

It was early fall when we reached there, and no big rainbows had been taken. "You may have to wait a few days more to hook 'em on the surface," the local experts said. "They still seem to down deep."

The evening was cold; a check on water temperature was favorable, and it seemed that the giant Kamloops should be coming to the top. Before dark, way out on the lake, I thought I saw a big one roll.

But two days of intensive fishing produced no large fish, and we had only one more day to spare.

Sitting on the porch on a bluff overlooking the lake that night, Joe chided me with an observation intended to start serious thinking. "You recently wrote a book called *Trout Waters*," he reminded. "It is about where to find big trout and how to catch them. If you don't know how to catch a big one here, your book can't be much good!"

Joe's remark caused me to spend a sleepless night trying to fit together information and facts I should have considered two days earlier.

At breakfast he regarded me with his usual affable smile. "Well, where do we go today?" he asked.

"I've been thinking it over," I answered, "and I'm sure the lake has turned over very recently, and I think we can take a big one on top. The Clark's Fork River evidently cuts a wide, curved channel out into the lake. If I were a big Kamloops, newly up from way down under, I would be in the lake where the current of the Clark's Fork comes in, waiting for bait to come down to me."

That morning we ran the boat in wide circles

in the current, sometimes trolling spoons on top; sometimes casting streamers or bucktails. Half an hour after arriving there the big one hit!

We didn't see the fish before he sounded deep, but he felt very heavy. After a few long runs he cruised slowly about; always staying twenty or thirty feet down. I kept all the tension on him that the tackle would allow, knowing that eventually something had to happen.

"Just a big Dolly Varden," someone commented but, hopefully, I thought otherwise.

After three quarters of an hour the constant tension took effect, and the big fish began to come up. Soon we could see him shimmering as he swam nearer to the surface, and finally he broke water, lying on his side, completely spent. The familiar pink stripe that identifies a rainbow trout decorated his sides.

"The net's too small for that one," the boatman said. "You'll have to gaff him."

"You do it," I said to Joe.

Joe expertly sank the gaff into the big rainbow's silvery side and grunted as his powerful arms swung him aboard.

The skipper pulled the throttles wide open, and the boat planed for the dock. "Let's weigh him right away," he said in explanation. "This one may be a record!"

The Kamloops weighed thirty-one pounds and twelve ounces, and would have gone a pound or so more if he could have been netted. It was a light-tackle record at the time. The world record of thirty-seven pounds still stands, but evidently the fish was caught by deep trolling with heavy tackle.

Figure 24. The author, with help from Joe Brooks, lands 31-pound, 12-ounce Kamloops on Lake Pend Orielle.

These two incidents point out that one can learn from books and from experience the general facts of water-reading lore. But all this isn't quite enough. To be successful one should adapt the pertinent facts to the situation at hand to obtain best results.

Northern Pike

Many cold- and cool-water lakes contain northern pike, which are so voracious that they often predominate to the near exclusion of other species. The pike is a spring spawner which often travels up rivers for the purpose. They feed during daylight hours, usually in early morning and late afternoon, with a period of inactivity around midday. While trollers often will catch pike almost anywhere in lakes frequented by them, this author has found them most often in spring and fall in shallow coves or close to weed beds. In temperatures higher than 65 degrees in summer they usually go deep, but rarely in water exceeding twenty feet.

Under such conditions we have seen fishermen use heavy wobbling spoons, with the result that they chiefly catch weeds and often get hung up. In shallow water, and often out deeper, use plugs which float when inactive and which pull under while being retrieved. Many readers will consider northern pike to be highly desirable gamefish, but the author is not among them. He thinks they are easy to find, to hook, and to bring in. They seem to show the most activity after one takes them from the water.

Dam Pools

While discussing cold-water lakes let's not forget the dams at their outlets, if they have any, and especially the pools below them. When logs collect around the upper part of a dam the protection thus afforded can provide excellent fishing by casting surface lures close to the logs or by drifting bait below them.

In fishing pools below dams, the water currents provide the keys to the main hotspots. For example, let's look at the famous Upper Dam Pool, in Maine's Rangeley Lakes area, which is typical of many insofar as water currents are concerned. The two gates at the left are open, as shown both in Figure 26 and in the photograph, thus pouring white water through the dam into the big pool at the left. Big fish usually lie in the moderate flow near the fast white water because this water is newly oxygenated and because food is brought down by the current.

The fast current flows down to the outlet, where it splits. The main part flows down the outlet, but part of it swings to the right and returns toward the dam, thus making a big eddy. One of the best fishing spots is where the current splits. On the right are two rocks, but many others are on the bottom, affording an excellent holding position where there is moderate flow, reasonable depth, and protection. Large salmon lie here.

As the smaller part of the current returns toward the dam, it provides very moderate flow

Figure 25. Upper Dam Pool, Rangely, Maine, a famous spot for lunker brook trout and landlocked salmon.

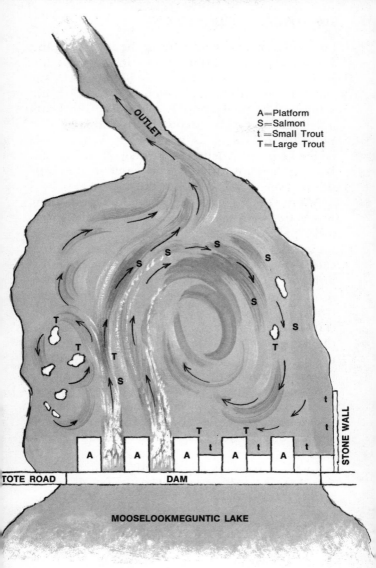

Figure 26. Diagram of Upper Dam Pool.

and a haven for smaller trout beside the stone wall on the right. Trout also lie in the moderate flow on the downstream sides of the rocks on the left, but this water evidently is too slow for salmon. The pool normally is fished from boats anchored where the current splits and from this point toward the rocks on the right. When a fish is hooked, the anchor is pulled, allowing the boat to drift into the quieter water in the middle of the eddy.

Many years ago, when fishing at Upper Dam was better than it is now, there was a small sawmill, part of which extended over the water, under the dam, where the stone wall is indicated at lower right. In the lower floor of the mill was a trap-door from which one could look into the water under the dam. The tremendous trout and salmon visible through the opened trapdoor, cruising in the darkened waters below the dam, were an angler's dream. They had coolness, protection, moderate flow, and a plentiful food supply—everything a fish could ask for. We used to fish as near as possible to the dam, and occasionally we would hook one of the big ones. When hooked, he quickly would snub the leader around one of the pilings of the dam, and break off.

Some of the very biggest fish lie in the protected water under dams, where it usually is impossible for anglers to catch them. Occasionally, however, they cruise out into the pool in the evening to feed. In cold-water lakes the early morning and late evening hours are the best ones for catching fish in pools below dams.

FISHING WARM-WATER LAKES

Warm-water lakes in southern regions differ from northern cold-water lakes in many ways other than their warmer temperatures and the different species and habits of fish that live in them. Many are man-made impoundments. While some are deep, generally they are shallow, without stratification, often containing bayous, swamps, sloughs, potholes, stumps, vast reedy expanses, rafts of hyacinths and other growths, and often are drained by canals. In addition to some of the basses and other pond fish found almost everywhere, they often contain species indigenous only to warm-water regions.

Cool-water lakes have some of the characteristics both of cold-water lakes and warm-water ones. They are the lakes "in-between" the two classes. Warm-water lakes usually are different enough from these so that we should treat them specifically. Let's visit a few to see how to "read them" for better fishing success.

Our host at Hot Springs, Arkansas, produced a box of his favorite lures (which may or may not be the favorites of other anglers). He chose an undressed jig leaded in a tear-drop design and painted dark red, with a light-wire, round-bend No. 2 hook. Onto this he threaded the head of a red plastic worm, so that the jig blended in shape with the worm; only the bend and point of the hook protruded.

"I make these myself," he said, "because we lose a lot of them in the brush piles. But we get a lot of bass, too! Take a spinning rod with about eight-pound-test line. We'll spend the day on Lake Ouachita."

Whether Ouachita should be termed a cool-water lake or a warm-water lake makes little difference. It is a large man-made impoundment of about 40,000 acres which is very typical of many, so it should serve as a good example.

"We don't bother much with trolling here," my host said. "Crappies and bass collect around points of land and brush piles. We'll anchor off this point of land and extend casts, fanwise, until the area is covered. Then we'll move off the tip of the point, and we'll fish the other side of the point before we move on. Let the lure sink to the bottom, and then twitch it in very slowly—only an inch or so at a time, so it will appear to be crawling slowly along the bottom."

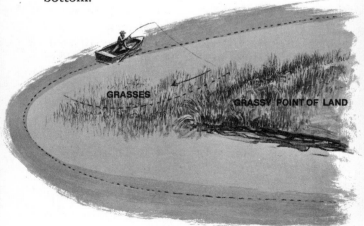

Figure 27. When fishing off a point of land, anchor boat at a distance (dotted line) and fish deep around point.

Following instructions, I let the leaded plastic worm sink, and twitched it in. There was an immediate strike, but the fish was off.

"Slower!" my guide cautioned. "The lure should barely be moving. And let the fish start off with it. You struck too soon. Just tighten up on him to be sure he has the hook. Then, if he hasn't, he may come back."

We took several fish around the point. "Keep only the big ones," my host advised. "We'll have enough before we go in anyway."

Leaving the point, we gunned the motor toward a brush pile whose dead gnarled tips formed a jumbled cluster above the surface. Looking down, we saw that the place was a maze of branches, stumps, and logs.

"Fish this the same way, only use shorter casts," I was advised. "You won't get caught up as often as you might think. When a fish has the lure, keep him coming to the top. Try not to give him a chance to snub the line around branches."

While working in the lure it became caught occasionally, but a twitch usually freed it. We managed to bring several bass or crappies to boat before getting so solidly hooked up that we had to break loose. Fish were plentiful. The points of land and the brush piles were the hotspots; so good, in fact, that we passed by many promising stumps and similar protective places that undoubtedly harbored fish.

(Crappies, members of the Sunfish family, are divided into two very similar varieties; the white crappie and the black crappie, the latter often being called calico bass.)

The next day we tried nearby Lake Hamilton, using somewhat different tactics. Hamilton also is a man-made lake, but of only about 4,000 acres in size and, unlike Ouachita, bordered with many stone walls protecting the lawns of homes. Swimming rafts and boathouses also provided havens for bass and pond fish.

Fishing here was much like the more heavily populated lakes of northern regions. Trolling along the stone-wall abutments in water only a few feet deep brought results, as did casts as close as possible to boat houses, rafts and other places where fish could find shade and protection. Here and there, points of land or rocky places along the shore proved effective.

Suddenly there was a flurry of action out on the lake. "White bass," the guide said, as he steered the boat there. Using small wobbling spoons, we caught several before the school sounded.

Man-Made Impoundments

The insatiable appetite of the U. S. Army Corps of Engineers for damming every waterway it can sweet-talk Congress into appropriating vast funds for, often without regard for common sense or ecological beauty, may be doing more harm than good; this depending on who is furnishing an opinion and why he is providing it. Whole towns often are removed and their people displaced against their will in order to furnish areas for dam impoundments. The main thing that can be said of some of the projects which many consider exorbitant and unnecessary is that usually they contribute to good fishing.

Such places provide a valuable water-reading tip for anglers. The areas have been mapped, and the maps are valuable to fishermen even though the former stream beds, roads, culverts, and so on now are under water. If such an impoundment is nearby, why not obtain a contour map of the area as it formerly was, and chart the water depths that now exist? If the bed of an entering stream is charted, it may be an excellent trolling area. An underwater bridge or culvert may be a haven for the "big ones." Ledges and submerged promontories may now be excellent feeding grounds for whatever species of fish have been introduced, including striped bass, which we used to think of as being purely a saltwater fish.

In fishing large and deep impoundments one may have to include depth-finding equipment on the boat in order to find his way around, but such equipment can locate former roads, bridges, heights of land, and other submerged characteristics, many of which now should be hotspots!

Farther to the south, as in Florida, shallow natural lakes and man-made impoundments abound. Here and to the west, farm ponds, flood-control and desert reservoirs, and lakes made by hydroelectric dams often abound with warm-water pond fish and gamefish, the big brother of which is the largemouth bass. While smallmouth bass are prevalent in most northern and southern states east of the Mississippi, except in far southern states, the largemouth is found in every state in the Union.

Shallow Lakes

Seekers of the largemouth find him most often in shallow, weedy lakes and river backwaters where he finds food and protection in and edging aqueous rooted vegetation; usually in waters not over twenty feet deep. Largemouths spawn in the late spring. In the North they weigh in the two- to three-pound range, rarely exceeding ten pounds or so. A subspecies, called the Florida bass, comes much bigger; in the five- to ten-pound range, sometimes weighing as much as fifteen pounds or more. This cousin of the largemouth spawns during most months of the year. Both have similar residential characteristics.

Thus, in general, the water reader looks for largemouth and Florida bass along grassy shorelines or near the edges of weed-beds in lakes.

In these shallow lakes, weedy flats (*Figure 28*) are productive if surface weedless lures are used. There is much more plant life under the surface than shows on top. When it's very hot the fish are found here only in late evening or early morning if deeper water is available for them to go to around midday. These flats usually are of wadeable depth and often are susceptible to excessive algae growth, which can spoil the fishing temporarily.

A poor place, which nevertheless often is fished by anglers, is a hyacinth line—the edge of a hyacinth bed. These floating weeds can be good fish cover, but when they are too plentiful they can ruin fishing as well as the bass habitat. When poisoned repeatedly they form a sludge on the bottom which reduces their fishing value. While hyacinth beds should be checked if they

Figure 28. Weedy flats are hotspots for big bass on southern lakes.

Figure 29. Hyacinth line is often a poor fishing spot. When weeds get too plentiful, they ruin bass habitat.

are handy, they are not as reliable as other forms of cover.

In shallow southern lakes, "reading the water" usually means "reading the weeds" because big bass usually are in them or on their edges. It also means finding potholes; fishing around stumps and cypress knees in the swamps, and in oxbows or bayous offering protective places such as have been described.

Rivers and Canals

In these regions, short rivers or drainage canals are so much a part of the shallow lakes that they should be included here. In southern rivers and canals we find masses of lily pads (known as "bonnets") as illustrated in *Figure 30*. These often grow in bands of varying width some distance from the shoreline. The strip of water between the bonnets and the bank often is very productive of all sorts of gamefish. The crappie shown was caught in chilly weather on a small spinning lure. The water on the far side of the pads generally is deeper, but it may be as deep as six to eight feet inside the pad line. Southern crappie are easiest to take in late winter and early spring. Bluegills (bream) also are found in the pads or just inside or outside of them. Schooling bass often will chase bait very near the line on either side. This picture shows a river situation, which differs somewhat from the patches of bonnets found in lakes, but fishing either pad lines or pad clusters is very much the same.

Flood-control canals connect or drain many southern lakes, some being dammed where they

Figure 30. Bands of lily pads, often found in southern rivers and drainage canals, are good places to fish for bass, bluegills, or crappies.

flow into salt or brackish water to afford salt-water fishing for snook, baby tarpon, and other species on the saltwater side of the small dam and freshwater fishing for bass and pond fish on the other. *Figure 31* shows a typical kind of bass and panfish water in southern Florida. It is a flood-control canal and this sort of water-way, on the marsh side in the foreground, usually contains a dense stand of cattails, sawgrass, lily pads, or other vegetation. These canals are of fairly recent origin and provide what their exponents like to call "conservation areas"; simply shallow impoundments built to conserve water and to prevent flooding. Typically, the canal itself may be quite deep, but the water may be very shallow on the marsh side, depending on the amount of water being held by the

Figure 31. The marsh side of flood-control canals can be good bass and panfish water.

impoundment. The other side is the dike side, and usually presents a steep drop-off. In cool weather the marsh side can be especially productive because it contains considerable submerged growth in addition to what is visible on top. There are many miles of canals like this in Florida.

Cypress Swamps

Another type of canal in southern regions is one which borders a cypress swamp, as shown in *Figure 32*. Such canals support wide varieties of vegetation and thus are havens for panfish and bass. The best time to fish them is when the swamp has almost drained and baitfish have been forced to leave the swamp for the canal proper. The near side of this ditch is shallow because the dike is set well back from it. Water depths vary on the other side, providing some places where airboats or light skiffs can penetrate the swamp.

Water Temperature

Although there are cold spells even in the Deep South, paying strict attention to water temperatures is no where near as critical as it is farther to the north. Temperatures in Gulf coast states average between 65 and 70 degrees, which is about in the middle of the ideal range for large-

Figure 32. Canals bordering cypress swamps provide good fishing as well as waterways for skiffs and airboats.

mouth bass, yellow bass, white bass, drum, channel catfish, warmouth, spotted bass, crappie, and other species of the Sunfishes which provide great sport in areas such as northern Florida and Louisiana.

Backwater Ponds

In Louisiana and other states bordering the Mississippi River one finds somewhat different fishing situations than have been discussed, such as backwater ponds. These are shallow lakes which receive backwaters from nearby rivers when they are in flood. Fast-flowing streams, usually lacking the rocky stretches found in northern ones, also provide excellent fishing. Being fed by springs and seepage, many of them are swift and usually clear.

Different situations usually pose no problems for anglers who are competent water readers and who are fishing far from home, because the requirements of individual species of fish are pretty much the same everywhere. It is true that bass, for example, may become acclimated to greater activity in warm waters of the South than they would be when exposed to the same temperatures in the North, but these differences are minor. One does not have to read thermometers exactly, because the general range of tolerable temperatures for each individual species is what counts. Bass evidently care little whether they are finding their food in the protection of northern lily pads and rushes or of southern hyacinths and sawgrass. It is the need for food and protection that counts, so "bassy spots" are rather similar everywhere.

INDEX

119